# Chi

## My Heritage - A Testimony

*Ten Miscarriages, Three Babies*

*[signature]*

*Esther Ota*

# Esther A. Ota

**outskirts press**

*I dedicate this book to my Lord and Saviour Jesus Christ.
He turned my mourning into dancing and gave me
the most amazing children in the world.
Indeed, weeping may endure for a night,
but joy comes in the morning.
To Him alone be all the glory and honour.*

# Table of Contents

# Acknowledgements

I first want to thank the Almighty God, who by the inspiration of the Holy Spirit enabled me to write this book. To Him alone be all the glory and adoration.

I honour my Prophet, the Presiding Bishop of Living Faith Church Worldwide, aka Winners' Chapel Inc., an anointed servant of God. The Lord sent His word into you and it has lighted upon me and loosed me from captivity. I also thank you for the Liberation Mandate, which translated into the Africa Gospel Invasion Project (AGIP). It was under this project that the late Pastor David Adams was deployed to The Gambia in 1995, by the Living Faith Church Worldwide, thereby giving me the opportunity to have encounters with prophecy, which triggered supernatural breakthroughs in my life.

Papa, I am eternally grateful.

The support and promptings of my dear husband, Dr. Martin Okechukwu Ota, through the production of this book is cherished. His input in typesetting the book, despite his busy work schedule, is deeply appreciated. My God reward you in return.

The unconditional love, unrelenting support, and encouragement of my wonderful children, John, David, and Restore, cannot be quantified. They also contributed immensely in typesetting this book. God indeed brought you to wipe away my tears. I give Him praise.

I appreciate my late parents: my father, Omeroha Inyang Eleje, and my beautiful mother, Ezinne Beatrice A. Eleje. You were an amazing and impenetrable team who gave me a loving, peaceful, stable, and solid foundation to launch into enviable heights. You taught me to believe in myself and I would accomplish anything. Your labour was not in vain.

To my spiritual father, Pastor Moses O. Oyedele, who graciously produced the foreword for this book, I say, I am grateful. You, also, together with your wonderful wife, Pastor (Mrs.) Modupe Dayo Oyedele, painstakingly edited the book. My God will honour you in return, sir.

The role played by my mentor and spiritual father, Pastor Chibuike Nwafor, is highly recognized. You have been my pillar of support through many challenges. You not only proofread this book, but your unrelenting words of encouragement spurred me on to its logical conclusion. I am grateful, sir.

I remain eternally grateful to my siblings: Sir Ifeanyi Eleje and his wonderful wife Lady Priscilla Eleje. I call you my parents and the unmovable duo because you have been there for me through thick and thin. God bless you abundantly.

To my ever-loving big sisters, Mrs. Immaculata Oko, Mrs. Florence Ononiwu, Dr. (Mrs.) Beatrice Onyeador, and Mrs. Rebecca Elenwo, I say thank you. Your contributions as well as moral and spiritual support are unrivaled. The support of my brothers, Dr. Austin Eleje, Mr. William Eleje, and Chief Edward Eleje, is also highly acknowledged. You are all amazing.

To my mentor, brother, and good friend, Hon. Justice Emmanuel Akomaye Agim (JSC), I say thank you. You have never stopped believing in me or my ability to achieve anything I aspire to. For countless times through the years you urged me to write this book. Your persistent promptings have paid off.

The support of my dear friend, Mrs. Augustina Omosigho, and her husband Mr. Edobor Omosigho, is also highly recognized. You are the best.

To every other person who contributed in one way or another in the production of this book, I am grateful. God bless you all.

# Foreword

The future looked so bright and promising. The euphoria of getting married at an early age without any medical challenge and more so getting married to a well-trained medical doctor, made the expectation of giving birth to two boys and a girl a solid reality. Not only that, two elder siblings who were well armed as qualified medical practitioners made unimaginable the thought of not being able to give birth to children as one would expect.

Then the revolving blows came with a big bang! The expectations seemed shattered. Miscarriages came upon miscarriages. In a nutshell, the devil had hit the author with the weapon of miscarriage ten solid times. Soon, the excitement of welcoming a new baby fizzled out and the expectations of the author and her husband to have three children as initially planned was becoming a mirage.

At a stage when it looked as if a breakthrough was coming, the devil struck again by presenting a long list of deadly diseases upon a child in the womb of the author. That verdict was pronounced via the mouths of some of the best doctors in one of the best hospitals in the world. Their conclusion was that she should flush out the baby in her womb.

Today, the devil was completely humiliated. Victory was given. Now Esther Ota and her husband are proud parents of two handsome and Holy Spirit-filled boys with a beautiful and God-fearing girl, to the glory of God. Vision fulfilled.

Reading *Children: My Heritage; A Testimony* is enough to stir up the spirit of anyone who is going through a similar situation to overcome the challenge of barrenness and miscarriages.

Testimony has the capacity to reproduce after its kind. The author painted a graphic picture of how she got her testimonies and she clearly demonstrated the path of faith she and her husband took to overcome the medical jargon that could deflate their faith and all the harassment of the devil that readers can employ to get out of the woods.

Do you know anyone facing a similar problem? Place a copy of *Children: My Heritage; A Testimony* in her hand; it is a miracle channel. Very soon, she will send you an invite to join her in the dedication of her children. With *Children: My Heritage; A Testimony*, your trial and travail shall surely turn to testimony.

Pastor Moses Oyedele, Senior Pastor
ROYAL CHAPEL,
BENIN CITY, NIGERIA

*And God said, let us make man in our image, after our likeness:*
*and let them have dominion over the fish of the sea, and over the*
*fowl*
*of the air, and over the cattle, and over all the earth, and over every*
*creeping*
*thing that creepeth upon the earth. So God created man in his own*
*image, in the*
*image of God created he him; male and female created he them.*
*And God blessed them, and God said unto them, be fruitful, and*
*multiply,*
*and replenish the earth, and subdue it: and have dominion over the*
*fish of the sea,*
*and over the fowl of the air, and over every living thing that moveth*
*upon the earth.*
**—Genesis 1:26–28**

# Backdrop

The institution of marriage was established by God as part of His order of creation with a definite blessing to the couple to be **"fruitful, and multiply, and replenish the earth, and subdue it: and have dominion"** *Genesis 1:28.* This is not just a blessing from God, it is also a command married couples are expected to obey. This command signals procreation.

So, married couples are ordained to procreate, which put in simple parlance is giving birth to children or bringing forth children. This is a heritage from God according to the book of Psalms:

> *Lo, children are an heritage of the Lord, and the fruit of the womb is his reward. As arrows are in the hand of a mighty man, so are children of the youth. Happy is the man that hath his quiver full of them, they shall not be ashamed but they shall speak with the enemies at the gate (Psalms 127:3-5).*

Merriam-Webster dictionary defines the word heritage, among others, as: (1) property that descends to an heir: something transmitted by or acquired by a predecessor, legacy, an inheritance, (2) something possessed as a result of one's natural situation or birth; birthright. Therefore, children are our inheritance, our birthright from God. It follows that God who is the owner of children has already made them available for us in the spiritual realm. It remains for us to possess them as our inheritance on earth.

It is clear from the scripture above that not only are children a heritage from God, they are also one of the instruments availed us by God with which to subdue and dominate the earth, as charged by God in **Genesis 1:28**. Therefore, the book of Psalms calls them arrows, signifying weapons, with which we wrath terror against the kingdom of darkness. They are ordained to operate in the supernatural, devastating the wicked devil and his cohort. That is why Prophet Isaiah declared: *"Behold, I and the children whom the Lord hath given unto me are for signs and for wonders in Israel from the Lord of hosts, which dwelleth in Mount Zion," Isaiah 8:18.*

Against this backdrop, it is also abundantly clear that our children are among the end-time army foreseen in the book of Joel in the following order:

*A day of darkness and of gloominess, a day of clouds and of thick darkness, as the morning spread upon the mountains: a great people and a strong; there hath not been ever the like, neither shall be any more after it, even to the years of many generations. A fire devoureth before them; and behind them a flame burneth: the land is as the garden of Eden before them, and behind them a desolate wilderness; yea, and nothing shall escape them.*

*The appearance of them is as the appearance of horses; and as horsemen, so shall they run. Like the noise of chariots on the tops of mountains shall they leap, like the noise of a flame of fire that devoureth the stubble, as a strong people set in battle array. Before their face the people shall be much pained: all faces shall gather blackness. They shall run like mighty men; they shall climb the wall like men of war; and they shall march everyone on his ways, and they shall not break their ranks: Neither shall one thrust another; they shall march everyone in his path: and when they fall upon the sword, they shall not be wounded. They shall run to and fro in the city; they shall run upon the wall; they shall climb up upon the houses; they shall enter in at the windows like a thief.*

*The earth shall quake before them; the heavens shall tremble: the sun and the moon shall be dark, and the stars shall withdraw their shining: And the LORD shall utter his voice before his army: for his camp is very great: for he is strong that executeth his word: for the day of the LORD is great and very terrible; and who can abide it. (Joel 2:2–11)*

The foregoing scripture epitomizes dominion. Great men and women that flow seamlessly to breakthroughs, on the substratum of visions and revelations. That shall be the lot of our children in Jesus' name. Amen!

# The Fall of Man

The question is: if children are our heritage, then, why are some barren and some suffer miscarriage?

My simple answer to this poser, is: ***"An enemy hath done this" Matthew 13:28.*** I say this because after God created man and woman, blessed them, and placed them in the garden of Eden, which is their place of perfection, the scripture has it that they sinned against God. Consequently, God cast them out of Eden into the outer world, a place of imperfection, to be tempted, plagued, and buffeted by the devil and his host of demons **(Genesis 3:1–24)**. That is why God said to man after the fall, *"You shall surely die."*

This is spiritual death, fall from grace to grass, from the heavenlies to the lowest of lows, at the mercy of the devil. So, stripped of his spiritual covering and defense, man was constrained to exist in his own strength, susceptible to the kingdom of darkness. This is fatal, because things of the spirit, such as the devil's operational realm, only answer to the spirit, which man had lost to sin.

God had a glorious plan for humanity, but when man sinned and disobeyed God he opened the door to the temptations and torments of the devil. It is important to note that God does not tempt any one: ***"Let no man say when he is tempted, I am tempted of God: for God cannot be tempted with evil, neither tempted he any man," James 1:13.***

There's no doubt that God can allow man to be tempted. You see that in the account of Job. Job's sufferings made him stronger in faith, even in the midst of his afflictions. He refused to sin. Consequently, his latter end was greatly increased **(Job 24:10)**.

It is the devil that tempts people. In the face of temptation, man has a choice: either to sin (drawn away by his own lust and enticed like in **James 1:14**) and thereby invite curses, or to resist sin and enjoy eternal life. It is a choice, according to the book of Deuteronomy: *"I call heaven and earth to record this day against you, that I have set before you, life and death, blessing and cursing: therefore, choose life, that both thou and thy seed may live," Deuteronomy 30:19.*

It follows that when man sinned he chose curses and death, the habitat of darkness. In line with this choice God pronounced curses upon the woman in this fashion*: "Unto the woman he said, I will greatly multiply thy sorrow and thy conception; in sorrow thou shalt bring forth children," Genesis 3:16a.*

This scripture has ofttimes been only associated with the pains of labour in childbearing. While I agree with this interpretation, to my mind, the scripture also signifies the sorrow of barrenness and miscarriages. These devilish manifestations work great torments in marriages, constantly defeating our marital bliss. Therefore, with sin and disobedience, childbearing ceased to be our heritage. It became an activity we have to labour for. Unfortunately, this consequence of rebellion has remained with mankind through generations. This is the reason why many, even in the household of faith, are barren, suffer miscarriages, and die during childbirth.

# The Divine Remedy

*For God so loved the world, that he gave his only begotten Son, that whosoever believeth in him should not perish, but have everlasting life.*
*—John 3:16*

The death and resurrection of Jesus repositioned man for dominion in the race of life. Once we become born again by accepting Jesus as our personal Lord and Saviour, our sin is blotted out and we become a new creature. This new status is as evidenced by **2 Corinthians 5:17–19:**

*Therefore, if any man be in Christ, he is a new creature: old things are passed away; behold, all things are become new. And all things are of God, who hath reconciled us to himself by Jesus Christ, and hath given to us the ministry of reconciliation; To wit, that God was in Christ, reconciling the world unto himself, not imputing their trespasses unto them; and hath committed unto us the word of reconciliation.*

Also, salvation rescues us from the curses of the law and the hold of Satan. This is because when Jesus was hung on the cross, He took upon himself the curse of our wrongdoing. Therefore, the book says: *"Christ hath redeemed us from the curse of the law, being made a curse for us: for it is written, cursed is every one that hangeth on a tree," Galatians 3:13.*

It follows that salvation is an escape route from darkness to life. No man is really living until he is saved. Without salvation we remain in the domain of darkness at the mercy of the devil and his agents from the pit of hell. It is salvation that gives us real life. See what the Bible says about this truth: *"He that believeth on the Son hath everlasting life: and he that believeth not the Son shall not see life; but the wrath of God abideth on him," John 3:36.*

Having taken us from darkness to light, salvation repositions us for our inheritance, including the heritage of children that was lost when man fell. This position is elegantly captured by the book of Acts of the Apostles as follows: *"To open their eyes, and to turn them from darkness to light, and from the power of Satan unto God, that they may receive forgiveness of sins, and inheritance among them which are sanctified by faith that is in me," Acts 26:18.*

That is why the scriptures say we are seated in heavenly places with Christ Jesus and have principalities and powers under our feet **(Ephesians 2:5–6).** In this highly exalted position we have power to trample upon serpents and scorpions and all the forces of darkness to enter into our promised land **(John 10:19).**

These redemptive packages are available for us to take delivery of once we become born again. However, delivery is not automatic. It is our clear understanding of our redemptive right and radical spiritual posture that puts us in command of our inheritance. If after being born again we continue to wallow in the realm of lack of knowledge and understanding, we will still suffer the torments of the devil.

# My Testimony

*I will speak of thy testimonies also before Kings,*
*and will not be ashamed.*
*—Psalms 119:46*

# CHAPTER 1

# Many Afflictions

*Many are the afflictions of the righteous; but the Lord deliv-*
*ereth him out of them all. He keepeth all his bones; not one*
*of them is broken.*
**Psalms 34:19–20**

I AM ONE of the women that went through trials and tribulations to
have children. God prevailed. I am now the proud mother of three
wonderful children. Thank God. It was not easy. It was a hard experience from which I drew some lessons. There is an advantage in every
problem in life. It takes understanding to see it. Challenges, if utilized
properly, birth changes in our lives. If only we could find a sense of
purpose in every challenge, we could discover God's plan and purpose for our lives.

I got married traditionally on 12 September 1992. Thereafter, we
conducted a civil wedding at the Court Registry in Port Harcourt,
Rivers State, Nigeria, on 17 September 1992. Even though I was sup-
posedly born again then, an event that occurred in 1988, whilst I
was still a student, I had not understood the full import of being born
again. I did not actively belong to any believing church. We were
thus content with the legal marriage conducted. To my mind this was
sufficient. We, however, took a very spiritual step after our marriage
even though we did not grasp the full purport of such a step. We knelt

down in prayer and asked God to give us three children: two boys and a girl.

A month after our marriage, I discovered I was pregnant. I was very excited, counting my blessings for the speedy gift of the fruit of the womb. I was still young, twenty-six years old then, and I also had the added advantage of the fact that my husband is a medical doctor. He also has a lot of friends who are obstetricians. I felt very secure by the fact that I was surrounded by medical personnel, including my two older siblings who are also medical doctors. In my little mind, what could possibly go wrong?

I was wallowing in ignorance, conceptualizing the forces of life in terms of the physical only, completely oblivious of the supernatural. I ignored the word of God and its potency in my life. I was to pay dearly for this ignorance. No wonder the Bible says *: "My people are destroyed for lack of knowledge: because thou hast rejected knowledge, I will also reject thee, that thou shalt be no priest to me: seeing thou hast forgotten the law of thy God, I will also forget thy children," Hosea 4:6.*

A very ominous warning, somewhat repeated by Prophet Isaiah in the following language *"Therefore my people are gone into captivity, because they have no knowledge: and their honourable men are famished, and their multitude dried up with thirst," Isaiah 5:13.-*

The scriptures above aptly capture who I was. Even though I professed to be born again in those days, an event that should have subjected the devil and his wiles under my feet, I had little or no knowledge of God and His word. Even the little I had been taught I put completely aside, trusting on human strength to triumph in life. So, I was a candidate for the harassment of the devil, who held me in captivity in the area of childbirth, because, *"by strength shall no man prevail," 1 Samuel 2:9.*

Therefore, the devil moved in on my first pregnancy when I was barely two months gone. I went to work one fine day in Lagos, Nigeria, where I was then resident, and just started bleeding. I had no contraction and no pelvic pain yet the blood kept coming out of me.

My husband was far away in Port Harcourt, where he was resident. My office called an ambulance and I was rushed to the hospital. On getting there, the doctors, after examining me, quickly moved me into the theatre and evacuated the womb. According to the doctors, that was the only intervention as the case was impossible. Beloved, I was hopeful that once I got to the hospital the doctors would intervene and save the baby. The arm of flesh completely failed me as demonstrated by scriptures:

> **Thus saith the LORD; Cursed be the man that trusteth in man, and maketh flesh his arm, and whose heart departeth from the LORD. For he shall be like the heath in the desert, and shall not see when good cometh; but shall inhabit the parched places in the wilderness, in a salt land and not inhabited. (Jeremiah 17:5–6)**

I was completely devastated. I remained on admission in the hospital for some days, heavily sedated. I remember waking up intermittently. I was informed by my minders that each time I woke up, I would cry, "My baby, my baby!" and I would be sedated all over again. My husband had to come down to Lagos from Port Harcourt to console me.

Shortly after this, in early 1993, my husband secured a contract with The Royal Victoria Hospital, Banjul, The Gambia, and relocated to The Gambia. A few weeks after his departure, I discovered that I was about six weeks pregnant. I employed all human efforts to ensure the preservation of this pregnancy. I saw my doctors regularly, did no strenuous job or exercise, took all the precautions and medication. All my efforts proved abortive. Why? Because: **"The labour of the foolish wearieth every one of them, because he knoweth not how to go to the city," Ecclesiastes 10:15.**

I did not apply the right know how. I did not have the right principle or technique to fight the devil. I was fighting a spiritual battle in the energy of the flesh. The adversary swooped in and terminated the pregnancy. Just as in the first pregnancy, I started bleeding at two months, was rushed to the hospital, and within a few hours I was taken into the theatre and my womb evacuated. The devil had won again, leaving me with an empty feeling, a sinking feeling, in the pit of my stomach.

## The Gambia

In an effort to cheer me up, my husband arranged for me to visit The Gambia. Therefore, in June 1993 I proceeded to The Gambia on vacation. This was my second time in another African country. My first trip was to Togo some years prior. I had visited Togo with my mother and two sisters in preparation for the upcoming wedding of one of my elder sisters. The trip to The Gambia was a different and more exciting experience. My husband met me at the airport and took me to his apartment in a place called Serrekunda. Though a densely populated neighbourhood, the apartment was located in a private compound, which also housed a bigger building occupied by the landlord, his beautiful Senegalese wife, and their three children. I soon fell in love with the landlord's family, especially the Senegalese wife.

She was a tall and imposing figure, given to the exotic fashion only peculiar to the people of the Senegambia region. She had a small boutique in front of the premises where she sold female clothing and accessories. It was a thriving business. We soon nicknamed her *"tuti tuti"* a Wolof word which loosely translated means "small small." This was because of her copious use of the phrase *"tuti tuti"* when speaking.

Tuti welcomed me very warmly. The Senegambia people are known for their hospitality. This came to the fore immediately upon my arrival in the premises. Tuti and her children evaded my home bearing all sorts of exotic dishes. There was *Benachin*, a rice dish which Nigerians and Ghanians call *Jolof rice*, aptly named because of the origins of the dish, which is traceable to the Wolofs or Jolofs of the Senegambia region. There was *Chicken Yassa*, a concoction made with chicken, plenty of onion, and other spices such as ginger, garlic, lemon, mustard, and black pepper to mention but a few. She also brought *Soupa kandja* aka okra soup. For dessert she served *Naan Mburu*, a rice pudding. It was a real feast. I was overwhelmed. She continued with this tradition for the duration of my one-month vacation in The Gambia.

I reciprocated by assisting her with sales in her boutique. Usually, I would follow my husband to work at the Royal Victoria Hospital. This afforded me the opportunity of visiting the famous Albert Market on Wellington Road, Banjul, take in the sights, and purchase some souvenirs for people back home in Nigeria. All other days I spent in Tuti's boutique. From this venture, I picked up a little of the Wolof language because Tuti spoke very little English, which is the lingua franca of The Gambia. Coming from Senegal, her lingua franca was French.

Consequently, she spoke mainly Wolof with her clients, which worked in my favour. I was never idle, which helped to distract me from my miscarriages. Tuti was also very encouraging and supportive. She shared some of her own experiences with me. She would always say to me in her limited English, "Don't worry, Esther; they will come," referring to children.

Prior to my arrival in The Gambia, my husband had submitted my resume to the Judiciary of The Gambia when vacancies were declared for magistrates. My vacation coincided with when interviews were conducted for these positions. I attended and was successful. I was given a leeway by the Judiciary to resume work in September 1993, which enabled me return to Nigeria and tidy my affairs there. Consequently, I moved to The Gambia in September 1993 and was sworn into the office of a magistrate, with my first seat of office at the Banjul Magistrates' Court. Given that my new office included a government accommodation, we moved from our home in Serrekunda to Cape Point, where the new residence was located. I was very sad leaving my home in Serrekunda and all my friends behind. I remained a frequent visitor in that neighbourhood for the duration of my sojourn in The Gambia.

Cape Point had its advantages. It was a very quiet neighbourhood by the sea. There was the Bakau market and other supermarkets within a walking distance from our residence. Most importantly, there was the Star of the Sea Catholic Church opposite the Bakau market. My husband and I had not been going to church. Since my husband was a Catholic by birth, we began attending the Catholic Church. Going to church also afforded us the opportunity of socializing with others in the Bakau/Fajara community, especially the Nigerian Expatriates, then working at The Medical Research Council Laboratories, UK (MRC), stationed in Fajara, The Gambia.

In 1994, I became pregnant again. The pregnancy had no chance against the devil because fear of miscarriage had crept into my life. As Bishop David Oyedepo always emphasizes, fear is a demonic spirit out to defeat our God given spirit of power, of love and of a sound mind **(2 Timothy 1:7)**. These are all attributes of the Holy Spirit at work in a believer. Therefore, fear is a torment. It kills. It is also the cheapest way to lose to the devil because, a man is a victim of what he fears. This is because fear is an expression of lack of faith in God and without faith it is impossible to please God **(Hebrews 11:6)**. Fear is also an expression of our expectation. What you fear is what you expect to happen in your life because expectation determines manifestation. Accordingly, the Bible says that the expectation of the righteous shall not be cut off **(Proverbs 23:18)**. Little wonder Job the sufferer posited: *"For the thing I greatly feared is come upon me, and that which I was afraid of is come unto me," Job 3:25.*

This is Job lamenting the consequences of fear upon his life. The book of **Job 1:8** records that Job was perfect, upright, feared God, and eschewed evil. Despite these sterling qualities, Job was so fearful that he constantly sanctified his children and offered burnt offerings on their behalf, lest they offend God and bring him into disfavour with God. His fear broke down the hedge of protection around his life, giving the devil room to torment him endlessly and steal everything from him. Therefore, whatever a believer does not fear cannot befall him. So, the book of **Philippians 1:28** exhorts us not to be afraid of our adversaries, which include the devil and all satanic oppressions.

I was then not aware of the truth about fear that I captured above. Hence, I was wallowing in fear, which is just false evidence appearing real. I was actively looking for that false evidence. I would check my underwear repeatedly during the course of each day for evidence of blood signaling a miscarriage. Subconsciously, I was expecting a miscarriage. I was sick, vomiting endlessly, anxious, distressed, and listless. My employers, Judiciary of The Gambia, were sympathetic especially in the face of the previous miscarriages. They granted me two months leave of absence with pay to ameliorate the first trimester of the pregnancy.

In spite of all these measures, I began to bleed one day. I was rushed to the Royal Victoria Hospital. My husband's colleagues did all they could possibly do by way of medical intervention. It was fruitless. I was eventually wheeled into the theatre and my womb evacuated. Human strength and knowledge could not save the pregnancy because it is *"Not by might, nor by power, but by my spirit, saith the Lord of hosts," Zachariah 4:6.*

## Solmenization of Marriage

After this miscarriage, my husband and I decided to take our marriage before God. We so needed divine intervention in childbearing that we were convinced that taking our marriage before God would somehow bring this to pass. Consequently, we celebrated our church wedding on 3 September 1994, at the Star of the Sea Catholic Church, Bakau.

It was a glorious day. We had a lot of favour in the process of the wedding in accordance with God's decree that *"Whoso findeth a wife findeth a good thing, and obtaineth favour of the Lord," Proverbs 18:22.*

Due to my melancholy and the disillusionment borne out of my miscarriages, I didn't want a wedding reception. I just wanted to appear in church in my wedding gown, get God's blessing in the presence of one or two witnesses, take a few photographs to commemorate the day, and then go home. This was not to be.

Four days before the date we set for the wedding, my husband approached his boss at the Royal Victoria Hospital, Dr. Ayo Palmer, to ask for permission to be off work for two days to enable him to constructively put finishing touches to the wedding plans. When Dr. Ayo Palmer heard we had organized such a wedding, she was scandalized. Being the kindhearted person she is, she mentioned it to her parents, Dr. Samuel Palmer (owner of the popular West Field Clinic, The Gambia) and his lovely wife, Mrs. Rachael Palmer, both of blessed memory. They promptly called us and redefined the wedding. They offered to host the wedding reception in their premises, in Fajara. They asked us to go ahead and invite as many people as we wanted. Since we did not have a wedding card, not having planned for one, we got on the phone and called all the people we were acquainted with in The Gambia.

Though it was very short notice everyone responded positively. We also hurriedly arranged a best man, Mr. Yusupha Ceesay, a good friend of my husband's, and a chief bridesmaid, my dear friend Ms. Ndella Jallow. A friend of mine baked a phenomenal wedding cake. The Palmers organized a sumptuous wedding buffet from the high-profile Atlantic Hotel, Banjul. Uniformed waiters from the same hotel also waited tables at the reception. The Palmers transformed their premises into a fairytale land. All hands were on deck. In the end we had a lot of people, both high and low, at the wedding. It was a glorious day.

Given that we hadn't planned a full-blown wedding, we did not have proper wedding rings because our plan was that I should purchase our wedding rings from the United States of America (US), where I was billed to travel to a month after our wedding. So, in the interim, I had found a presentable ring from Albert market that fitted my finger perfectly, but not my husband. All efforts to find a presentable ring that would fit his finger proved abortive. We could not get one custom made because of the short notice. We resorted to buying a pair of cheap circular children's earrings which we modified into a wedding ring for my husband. The "ring" faded right in the church during the solemnization of the wedding, to our amusement and that of a few others who knew the history of the "ring." I, however, bought proper gold wedding rings, as intended, during my visit to the US a month after our wedding. The rings were duly blessed by the reverend father who wedded us. It is worthy of note that during this visit to the US, with the help of my older brother, Dr. Austin Eleje, who practices medicine in the US, I underwent a comprehensive medical checkup. I was given a clean bill of health, as nothing was found to be medically responsible for the frequent miscarriages.

In April 1995, my husband secured another appointment with the Medical Research Council Laboratories (MRC). The appointment came with a bigger house in a big compound and a much larger salary. We moved yet again from our home in Cape Point to the much larger residence in Fajara. We were slowly but surely moving up in life.

# CHAPTER 2

# I Was Mocked

*Looking unto Jesus the author and finisher of our faith; who for the joy that was set before him, endured the cross, despising the shame, and is set down at the right hand of the throne of God.*
*For consider him that endured such contradiction of sinners against himself, lest ye be wearied and faint in your minds.*
**—Hebrews 12:2–3**

LET ME INTERPOLATE at this junction, to capture some of the shame, reproach, contempt, scorn, ridicule, disdain, and derision I endured because of my childlessness. This, I recount without any form of bitterness, but to serve as a form of encouragement to those who may be going through a similar experience.

Success attracts envy. As a magistrate then, I had a few perks in the society and my husband was also making strides as a medical doctor. We were well sought after in our sector of the community to play vital roles in social events. I had become the envy of many and a favourite subject of gossip because of my miscarriages. As the Bible says: *"He had dispersed, he had given to the poor, his righteousness endureth forever; his horn shall be exalted with honour. The wicked shall see it and be grieved, he shall gnash with his teeth and melt away, the desire of the wicked shall perish," Psalms 112: 9–10.*

Accordingly, when you succeed or are honoured in life many people become envious and angry (grieved) of that success. This is the unfortunate reality of life. Sometimes people despise you, not because you have offended anyone, but just because they are grieved by what you represent—either your stature, outlook, associations, family background, or whatever spells honour in you. I speak from experience. I was born into a well-respected family, and have witnessed the anger of many because of that honour. God also lifted me from a magistrate to judge of the High Court and the Court of Appeal, President of the Court of Appeal, and justice of the Supreme Court, in a few Commonwealth jurisdictions. Consequently, I can authoritatively articulate the acrimony of some when one is honoured. It is fear and insecurity about the lifting of another person that breeds envy and jealousy. Therefore, being intimidated and afraid of your success and honour, others become envious and jealous. On the other hand, some covet what you have. This also leads to envy and jealousy: *"Let us not be desirous of vain glory, provoking one another, envying one another," Galatians 5:26.* Blinded by envy and jealousy, rather than admit your honour and celebrate you, they find every occasion to backbite and slander you.

## Scriptural Examples of Mockery

Mockery has been the order of creation from time immemorial. The examples of such occasions abound in scriptures. We will consider a few here. Jesus Christ our Lord and Saviour is a palpable example. It was because of envy of his honour that his detractors delivered him up to be crucified, not because of any wrongdoing on his part. The scripture acknowledges this fact as follows: *"For he knew that for envy they had delivered him," Matthew 27:18.*

The apostles also faced much envy and jealousy because of their success in the gospel of Jesus Christ. The Acts of the Apostles recounts one such occasion as follows:

*And some of them believed, and consorted with Paul and Silas, and the devout Greeks, a great multitude and of the chief women not a few. But the Jews which believed not moved with envy, took onto them certain lewd fellows of the baser sort, and gathered a company, and set all the city on an uproar, and assaulted the house of Jason, and sought to bring them out to the people. And when they found them not, they drew Jason and certain brethren unto the rulers of the city, crying, these that have turned the world upside down are come hither also; Whom Jason hath received: And these all do contrary to the decrees of Caesar, saying that there is another king, one Jesus. And they troubled the people and the ruler of the city, when they heard these things. (Acts 17:4-8)*

Daniel did not escape the wrath and grievances of his detractors, who sought to find occasion with him out of envy, because he was distinguished above all and had an excellent spirit upon him (**Daniel 6:1–28**). The same was the lot of Joseph who was sold into slavery by his brethren: *"And the patriarchs, moved with envy, sold Joseph into Egypt: But God was with him," Acts 7:9.*

There is also Cain who, driven by envy, killed his brother Abel (**Genesis 4:1–26**). Even the great prophet Elisha was mocked by small children who followed him crying, *"Go up thou bald head, go up thou bald head," 2 Kings 2:23.*

The cases are legion. The above will suffice in these circumstances. It is inexorable, from the examples detailed above, that the demonic spirit of envy and jealousy has plagued man from centuries back. The problem is that when this demon takes hold of a man, it manifests in such a fashion that no matter what the victim of envy does to mitigate it, the villain is largely not pacified. As the book of Proverbs recognizes: *"Jealousy is the rage of a man: Therefore, he will not spare in the day of vengeance. He will not regard any ransom, neither will he, rest content, though thou givest many gifts," Proverbs 6: 34-35.*

It follows from this scripture that giving, which is a show of love, oftentimes does not ameliorate envy and jealousy, because it is a spirit that can only be dealt with spiritually.

## My Experience

My case could not be ameliorated. I took copious steps to curb the envy. I ignored the pungent attitudes and obvious sniggering. I chose to embrace people, opening my home to many. This prompted me to accept to play important roles in activities in my community. Therefore, I accepted to play the role of wedding mother at weddings and godmother to newborn babies. I channeled my efforts, strength, and resources into these events. In most cases, the same people I served and honoured turned around to become my deadliest detractors.

There were myriads of such cases. One in particular struck a very raw cord. I had served as godmother of the first child of this particular couple. Shortly afterward, they had a second baby. During the dedication of the baby, I arrived at the couple's home bearing gifts as usual. When the track "Sweet Mother," by the popular Cameroonian-born singer Prince Nico Mbarga (deceased) began to play, the celebrant picked up her newborn baby and began dancing. All the other married women present, who incidentally all had children except me, took their children and joined her. I was left sitting. Since I had my godson on my lap, I carried him to the dance floor and joined in. To my utter horror, the celebrant hurried over to me, snatched my godson from my hands, and danced away muttering under her breath to the amusement of many present. The whole aim was to disgrace me publicly for no apparent reason other than envy. After all, as the godmother of that child, I am also technically his mother—a role I have played to the hilt. So the show of shame by his mother was unnecessary but for envy. As the Bible says: ***"For where envying and strife is, there is confusion and every evil work," James 3:16.***

My mother had advised me to be accommodating to people, especially children and pregnant women, as these acts of kindness would bring my own children. I keyed right into this wise counsel. Once someone I knew had delivered and I was informed, I would prepare a concoction, a delicacy called pepper soup. This is a hot soup made of various African spices used to sooth the womb after delivery. I carried pepper soup to everyone around me who had a baby, and they were many. We were then all at the childbearing age, so it appeared like everyone I knew was having babies. Consequently, I found myself carrying pepper soup all over the place.

Rather than gratitude, I was ridiculed and derogatorily nicknamed "Mama Pepper Soup," meaning "Mother of pepper soup." It was a name some audaciously called me to my face. Indeed, the heart of man is dangerously wicked.

I also tried to embrace many children, but most of the mothers were not welcoming. There was however one woman in the circle of my associates, a highly placed woman in the society, who had another spirit. Obviously, she had nothing to lose or to envy me for. I also believe she must have seen my heart and the longing in it. She, therefore, frequently left her two children in my care. Those children were my solace, my constant companions. Just caring for them helped me focus less on my own problems.

My detractors were soon to key in on this too, and began calling me names, such as "Nanny" and "Housemaid." In their little minds, my association with her was borne out of the fact that she was highly placed in the society—an argument that was seriously flawed, because, I too had a good position in the society.

In any case, I have always believed that while we teach those below us, we should also learn from those more successful than us. It takes humility to serve others, whether great or small, especially after you have achieved in your own rights. As Apostle Paul charged the Philippians: ***"Let nothing be done through strife or vainglory, but in lowliness of mind, let each esteem other better than themselves," Philippians 2:3.***

The above scripture resonates with me. It speaks directly into my perception of life, which is humanity. This has helped me maintain friends and associates all through different strata of the society. To me, great or small, we are all created in the image of God. Regrettably, many do not understand this.

Finally, I deem it expedient to mention what I term "household wickedness." That is the closest sort of vilification and the most difficult to endure. Unfortunately, this is the kind suffered by most women and the most painful to bear. Speaking about this kind of wickedness, the book of Matthew declares *"And a man's foes shall be they of his own household," Matthew 10:36.*

This kind of wickedness has been there from times long past. Hannah suffered it. In **1 Samuel 1:2-6**, Hannah who was barren was **"provoked sore"** by Phineas her co-wife, whom the Bible referred to as her adversary. It is important to know that household wickedness does not necessarily have to be from a relative. It could be from a close friend or associate who is regarded as a relative. Such a person also qualifies as a member of your household.

I encountered this sort of provocation. People I embraced as family and bought many gifts for strove to kill my spirit because of my childlessness. I soon discovered that some were also envious of all I stood for. Whenever I found myself in their presence, I felt the tension. Some looked me up and down with daggers in their eyes. Some passed unsavory, unnecessary, and unsustainable comments right to my face. The taunts and innuendos were not lost on me.

On one occasion that I had a miscarriage, one woman called me on the phone. Her mission was not to sympathize but to provoke. There was no sense of decency, solace, consolation, or humanity in her words to me. The import of her call was that she heard I had another miscarriage and in fact she didn't even know how to tell her mother such a thing. The whole attitude was that I had committed a crime by having another miscarriage. For the sake of peace, I endured all in silence, for: *"He that covereth a transgression seeketh love, but he that repeateth a matter separateth very friends," Proverbs 17:9.*

## The Purpose of Mockers

It is important that you understand the mission of mockers, to best grasp how to deal with them. Just like the devil, they have only one mission which is *"to steal, to kill and to destroy," John 10:10.* Mockers aim to bully and intimidate you, like the devil. They seek to judge you with their mockery, thereby distracting you from your purpose and vision with their wiles. They aim to make you feel worthless by attacking your self-esteem and self-confidence, so that you can denounce God. You forget that Jesus has completed the work for you and through faith in Him you can access your heritage in redemption. Having lost sight of who you are, you will become ashamed of yourself and your circumstances. In this state, you forget all the good things God has done in your life. This leads to frustration, and in many cases death. Some even mock your God, asking, *"Where is the word of the Lord? Let it come now," Jeremiah 17:15.* This can make you doubt God and his word, resulting in utter destruction. So, you eventually lose everything. God forbid!

## How to Deal with Mockers

First and foremost, realize there are no stars without a scar. That is why the Bible says, *"when* **we go through waters, rivers, fires,"** **(Isaiah 43:2)** and not *if* we go through those challenges. This scripture shows that trials will surely come but our assurance is that God is with us always.

Once you have this indisputable fact in place, then you are well positioned to adopt the best attitude to mockery, which is silence and endurance. Jesus Christ our Lord, who for the joy set before him endured our shame and reproach without complaining, according to the book of Hebrews, is our perfect example:

> *Looking unto Jesus the author and finisher of our faith; Who for the joy that was set before him endured the cross, despising the shame, and is set down at the right hand of the throne*

*of God. For consider him that endured such contradiction of sinners against himself, lest ye be wearied and faint in your minds. (Hebrews 12:2–3)*

Beloved, silence is golden. Silence is wisdom. Never reply to your mockers in anger, because you may speak foolish words like them, hence reducing yourself to their level. There is no doubt that everyone enjoys a fitting reply, however, it is wisdom to say the right thing at the right time. Rather than trade words with your mockers, pray for them, and God will honour you for that. Job's friends were his deadliest mockers. The Bible has it that even in the midst of their mockery Job prayed for them. God stepped in, turned Job's captivity, and his latter end was greatly increased **(Job 42:10).**

There is also no need complaining to anyone. Complaining may only make your case worse. This is because that person you think is your best friend may just be an enemy. The person you see as a trusted family member may just be your detractor. The devil can use anyone. Tell them your hurts and they promptly gang up with your mockers to mock you. They tell unprintable lies behind your back just to assuage their own envy and jealousy. It is also important to note that complaining and murmuring show lack of faith in God. This leads to utter destruction **(1 Corinthians 10:10).** Therefore, rather than go about complaining to man, who has no lasting solution and may betray you, why not take your case to Jesus? He never fails. He is the author and finisher of our faith and only His counsel will stand in our lives.

Apostle Paul understood this truth. He refused to succumb to the judgment and criticisms of man. He refused to judge himself based on man's mockery, opinion, or judgment. He clearly recognized God as the ultimate judge, who will judge us not on the outward appearance (which can be deceptive), but on the hidden things of darkness and the manifest counsels of the heart *(1Corinthians 4:3–5).*

Wisdom is profitable to direct. So, I bore all the mockery in silence, never complaining to anyone. I did not let my detractors discourage me from good deeds or steal my joy. I had a clear purpose and vision. Therefore, I persisted, knowing that at the appointed time God would turn their wicked mockery into great glory. I held onto this expectation.

# CHAPTER 3

# Remembering My First Love

*Nevertheless, I have somewhat against thee, because thou
hast left thy first love. Remember, therefore, from whence
thou art fallen, and repent, and do the first works; or else
I will come unto thee quickly, and will remove thy candlestick out of his place,
except thou repent.*
**—Revelation 2:4–5**

I WAS SOON to get pregnant again, a pregnancy I lost within a very short period of time. At a time in one's life there is need for introspection. Prior to the loss of the pregnancy, I had stopped going to church for about four months. I just could not be bothered. There was something deeply missing in my life. There was a disconnect with God and I just did not know how to reconnect.

As a growing child, I had witnessed my mother embrace the Pentecostal faith. She was a committed member of the Presbyterian church. However, being a person whose heart naturally panted after God, I guess she wanted more, which apparently engendered her to welcome the Pentecostal movement, which she was exposed to in the school where she was a teacher in Enugu, Nigeria. Consequently, she attended evening services in one Pentecostal church located in New Haven, Enugu, almost every day. Sometimes, she took my cousin, who was then living with us, and I, to these evening prayer meetings. She would always tell us that God had done great things for her and that we should always turn to God when faced with challenges.

I was to desperately turn to God a few years later in 1988, after my father died. I had some difficulties facing the realities of life after the demise of my father. I lived with my parents on Glover Road, in the highbrow Ikoyi neighbourhood, on Lagos Island, toward the later part of my father's life. All my activities were concentrated on Lagos Island. Whenever I had to go to the mainland, I was chauffeur driven by one of our family drivers. Consequently, I never took public transport to the mainland prior to my father's death. I had a very protective father whose family ideals have greatly impacted on me.

After the passing of my father, my mother chose to relocate to the Eastern part of Nigeria. We also gave up our residence in Ikoyi, which was tied to my father's job. So, whilst in the prestigious Nigeria Law School, Victoria Island, Lagos from 1988 to 1989, to complete my law studies I had to reside with the family of my best friend on Rumens Road, Ikoyi. Although my elder brother, Sir Ifeanyi Eleje, and his lovely wife, Lady Priscilla Eleje, were resident around Gbagada on the mainland in those days, this arrangement suited all of us because of the proximity of Ikoyi to Victoria Island, where the law school is located. However, I would go to my brother's house every weekend.

The first time I had to go to Gbagada using public transport was very challenging and led me to Christ. Up till this day, I still do not understand why I allowed my friends to dissuade me from taking a taxi (what Nigerians call drop) to Gbagada, even though I had enough money on me to do just that. The contention was that it would be an unnecessarily expensive venture and I agreed with them.

So, on the faithful day, my well-meaning friends gave me adequate descriptions on how to get to Gbagada by bus. Transportation in Lagos in those days was quite challenging, requiring some stops and bus changes, depending on your destination. After classes on that Friday, I went straight to a bus stop called CMS, which is like a central bus station in Marina, Lagos, where I boarded a bus for the mainland. I was to change buses twice before getting to Gbagada. When I got to the first bus stop where I was to change buses, it was already getting late, about 6:00 p.m. I got out of the bus and stood at the bus stop waiting for the right bus to come along. As the custom was in those days, every bus had a conductor who would step out at every bus stop, chanting the name of their next destination. I waited and waited at the bus stop, but did not hear my next destination being called out.

It was getting dark. I noticed a lady who was carrying a Bible. I presumed that she was either going to church or returning from one. I approached her to make enquiries. She informed me that I was on the wrong side of the road. She said I needed to cross the overhead bridge, a pathway for pedestrians, which spanned across the road to get to the other side. Apparently, I had boarded the wrong bus and was way off my destination.

She directed me to a nearby overhead bridge and advised me to hurry up and get out of that neighbourhood to avoid being robbed. That was when I realized I was sticking out like a sore thumb, and quite a number of people were staring at me. Given that I was coming directly from the law school, I was corporately dressed in a smart skirt suit, nice gold accessories, wearing my Raymond Weil wristwatch (one of my treasures in those days, I can't forget that watch!), stiletto heels, and carrying an expensive leather briefcase. I had just procured the whole ensemble from the US and the United Kingdom (UK), where I had been sent by my family that summer to buy my wig and gown from the prestigious Ede and Ravencroft, Chancery Lane, London, and also shop for other items in preparation for law school. Robbers could usually perceive any foreign entity from afar and I was screaming: "foreign!" I was a candidate for robbery.

Really terrified at that stage, I quickly hurried to the overhead bridge, climbed the steps, and got on the bridge. I have many strengths in life, but one of them is not heights. I could not make the trip across the bridge. I had a dizzy spell. Adrenaline began to pump in my head.

I was frozen at one spot and sweating profusely. I started crying as I imagined all sorts of harm befalling me.

Unknown to me, the kindly lady from whom I had earlier sought directions was watching me. When she noticed that I was not moving, she climbed the bridge to find out what was going on. I just kept crying, "Papa, Papa," calling for my late father. I was a miserable wreck, remembering all the perks I had enjoyed in life courtesy of my dear father. Somehow, I managed to tell my liberator that I had just lost my father that year and I had never crossed an overhead bridge before. She was very sympathetic and offered to help me across the bridge. I refused, too scared to make the crossing even with her help. She then told me that she was going to church and if I was minded to follow her, one of her church members who lived in the Gbagada area would take me home after the service.

Ordinarily, I would not follow a stranger anywhere, no matter the circumstance and no matter how angelic she appeared. However, on that day I readily agreed to proceed to church with her. I guess it was the Holy Spirit, the Lord of the harvest, compelling me to church, because I gave my life to Christ on that day and became born again.

So, in the midst of my frequent miscarriages, I began to introspect on my past experiences with the Pentecostal church, trying to reconnect a disconnect with God. My kindly mother was soon to add her voice to my miscarriages, telling me that they were spiritual attacks and not physical and that it was only God who could settle it. Consequently, my husband and I began to search for a Pentecostal church. They were not many in The Gambia in those days. Luckily, through a friend of ours we found one, Glory Baptist Church. Thus, in 1995, we left the Catholic Church and began worshipping at the Glory Baptist Church.

## Rededication to God

After my family moved to join the Glory Baptist Church, I rededicated my life to God. I tried to press into the Kingdom of God by attending church services frequently. There was a yearning in me to increase in spiritual strength. I read in the book that: ***"They go from strength to strength, every one of them in Zion appeareth before God," Psalms 84:7.*** So, I became a frequent churchgoer. I attended all church programs.

Since I desperately needed a miracle, I decided to do more. In those early days of my journey with Christ, I was able to grasp that prayer was one vital key to unlocking doors of captivity, such as the one that was holding me down. Though I did not fully comprehend the potency of prayer, I was still eager to put that to work. I decided that apart from praying with my husband, I needed to pray with another person, a prayer partner. According to the Bible: ***"Iron sharpeneth iron; so a man sharpeneth the countenance of his friend," Proverbs 27:17***

My understanding of this scripture in the context of a prayer partner was that such a prayer partner would advance the effectiveness of my walk with God. This is because some of the benefits of praying with a prayer partner are as follows:

1. It promotes selflessness, which is one of the principles that guarantee answers to prayers. This is due to the fact that it makes you lay aside your own problems and pray for others, which is a recipe for answered prayers. The Bible accounts that Job's circumstances changed when he prayed for his friends: ***"And the Lord turned the captivity of Job, when he prayed for his friends; also the Lord gave Job twice as much as he had before," Job 42:10.***

2. It promotes prayer of agreement, which is a very potent force. In fact, we are guaranteed by scriptures that such prayer of agreement in faith, will of certainty, be answered by God: ***"Again I say unto you, that if two of you shall agree on earth as touching anything that they shall ask, it shall be done for them of my Father which is in heaven. For where two or three are gathered together in my name, there am I in the midst of them," Matthew 18:19–20.***

3.  It helps you pray more frequently and consistently, thereby promoting accountability in your prayer life: *"Rejoice evermore, pray without ceasing. In everything give thanks: for this is the will of God in Christ Jesus concerning you,"* 1 Thessalonians 5:16–18.

4.  It helps others pray for you. Sometimes, you are down completely and lack the spiritual energy to pray. A prayer partner, if at hand, steps in, fills the gap, and pulls you up, as testified by the scripture below: *"Two are better than one, because they have a good reward for their labour. For if they fall, the one will lift up his fellow: but woe to him that is alone when he falleth; for he hath not another to help him up,"* Ecclesiastes 4:9–10.

Armed with the above understanding, I began to look for a prayer partner. I studied the women in the church. I needed a good friend, someone who genuinely loved and cared for me, that could tell me the truth and pull me up when I was down. I needed a genuine friend to pray in partnership and command open heavens. I did not need another detractor to pull me down spiritually, under the weight of gossips, envy, slander, and backbiting. I was soon to find a genuine relationship in a quiet, unassuming, responsible, caring, loving, and God-fearing woman, my sister and friend, Mrs. Augustina Omosigho. Sister T, as I fondly call her, is one of the rare creatures God planted on earth. Somehow, we gravitated toward each other. Sister T and her ever--loving husband, Mr. Edobor Omosigho, lived a quiet life, which suited me just fine. They currently reside in Dallas, Texas, US.

I was soon to discover that Sister T was also waiting on God for the fruit of the womb. We became, not just friends, but ardent prayer partners. It is worthy of note that the bond between us has fostered into sisterhood over the years and still subsists until this day. My Sister T was blessed with the fruit of the womb, a beautiful baby girl called Faith. She waited for nineteen years, but God who is too faithful to fail, answered her. She has since captured her experience in a book titled FROM BARRENNESS TO FRUITFULNESS, The Story of My Life.

# CHAPTER 4

# Days of Miracles

*And by a prophet the Lord brought Israel out of Egypt, and*
*by a prophet was he preserved.*
**—Hosea 12:13**

PRAYERS ARE POTENT and they provoke miracles. God Himself, speaking about prayers, proclaimed: *"Call unto me, and I will answer thee, and shew thee great and mighty things which thou knowest not," Jeremiah 33:3.*

The great and mighty things propounded by this scripture are miracles, which are strange acts of God provoked by the desperate faith of men. They are events translated from the supernatural, which become manifested in the physical to the astonishment of many.

I have always known that the supernatural exists. I have always had a connection with events yet to come, in an uncanny way. Sometimes, it comes by way of an intuition. Things drop into my mind and I will eventually see them playing out in the physical. This is how I always knew that my father would visit me whilst I was in secondary school at Federal Government Girls College, Bakori, in the Northern part of Nigeria. Then, my parents lived in Enugu, which is in the Eastern part of Nigeria. Unannounced, my father would come visiting outside the official school visiting days. I still have these intuitions.

However, the more potent spiritual makeup of my being are

dreams. My dream interludes are so strong that most times they become a reality. For example, I dreamt of my father's death for seven days in a row, the same scene each night. I was a nervous wreck. He was not sick. I even got the opportunity to ask him why he wanted to die and he laughed it off. Two weeks after this encounter, my father dropped dead in his bedroom. This was on 27 April 1988. I dreamt of my mother's passing too. I dreamt of the passing of other family members and friends. I also have positive dreams of promotions, births, etc. Suffice it to say that most events I dream of and recollect vividly on waking up invariably come to pass. However, with better understanding, I now reject the negative dreams as traps of the devil, thereby rendering them impotent.

I was soon to have a different sort of encounter with the supernatural, a kind I had only heard of, but never experienced. The days of miracles are still here. If you've never experienced one, it is hard to believe until it happens to you. Even though I was born again, I was still doubtful whether God actually speaks to people. So, in those days, when pastors and prophets say God spoke to them, a part of me would be like "seriously?" This just goes to speak to my level of Christianity and spiritual understanding at this stage of my life, until it happened to me.

## Encounter with Angels

I first heard of Living Faith Church, aka Winners' Chapel, from an acquaintance of ours, Mr. Eustace Opara, who also lived in The Gambia. He told us about some pastors from Winners' Chapel, who had been sent by Bishop David Oyedepo, the Presiding Bishop of Living Faith Church Worldwide, to The Gambia to win souls under the Africa Gospel Invasion Program (AGIP). Winners' Chapel did not have a church in The Gambia in those days. What the pastors did was organize outreaches and Bible schools where they would teach the gospel of Jesus Christ. The graduates of these outreaches and Bible schools were sent to different churches. The pastors would then visit one church after another on Sundays to follow up on these new converts.

27

We heard all this from Mr. Eustace Opara, who also told us that the pastors had suffered a lot of tribulation in The Gambia. They were labeled cultists, because of the use of the prophetic mantle and anointing oil—so much so that their host, a pastor of one of the churches in The Gambia, drove them away from his residence alleging that they were practicing African magic (aka juju). This was all we knew about Winners' Chapel until we encountered the pastors.

One Sunday, in November 1995, whilst my husband and I were in church at the Glory Baptist Church, Mr. Eustace Opara walked into the church with two very well-dressed gentlemen who we later learned were the Winners' pastors. I remember that day vividly. One of our close friends, a medical doctor, was relocating to Namibia with his family, and they were being sent forth by the church. The Winners' pastors were, however, not there for this send forth. They had come to follow up on some of the new converts and graduates from their Bible school, who they had sent to worship at the Glory Baptist Church.

Whilst praise was going on in the church service, Mr. Eustace Opara called out my husband and conferred with him. My husband, upon return back to where we were seated, wrote a note to me as the noise from the choir could not allow us to talk. In the note, he explained that the two men who came to the church with Mr. Eustace Opara were the Winners' pastors. He stated that Mr. Eustace Opara was requesting that since we were all Nigerians in a foreign land, it would have been good if we could offer to host the pastors to lunch that day after the church service, seeing they had faced a lot of tribulation in The Gambia. I readily agreed. I always had assorted food in the house, given that I love cooking and entertaining. I say this with all humility: my husband and I are natural givers, even though at this material point in time we had little understanding of the spiritual connotations of giving.

## Madam, Where Are Your Children?

Immediately after the service, we approached the pastors, who we later came to learn were Pastor David Adams and Pastor Wesley

Anzizi. We introduced ourselves to them and invited them to our home. Somehow, we found favour with them and they accepted. Therefore, we proceeded with them to our residence. I had no idea that I was about to entertain angels. As the Bible says: *"Be not forgetful to entertain strangers; for thereby some have entertained Angels unawares," Hebrews 13:2.*

I had taken angels into my home unawares! Behold, these are still the days of angelic visitation as was the case in the times past as accounted in the scriptures. I say this because what happened to us after entertaining these pastors in our home is akin to what happened to Abraham and Sarah, his wife, who was barren, evidencing the fact that giving provokes supernatural fruitfulness.

This account appears in **Genesis 18 and 21.** Abraham, sitting at the front of his house, saw three men standing before him. Abraham ran to meet them and bowed himself toward the ground. He offered to fetch water to wash their feet, a morsel of bread to comfort their hearts, and for them to take a rest under the tree. The men agreed. So Abraham and his wife, Sarah, prepared a good meal, set it before the three men, and "they did eat." After eating, the men said to Abraham: *"Where is Sarah, thy wife? And he said, 'Behold in the tent.' And he said, 'I will certainly return unto thee according to the time of life, and lo Sarah thy wife shall have a son,' " Genesis 18:9–10.*

This prophecy was fulfilled in **Genesis 21:1-2**, where God visited Sarah and did unto Sarah as he had spoken. Sarah conceived, and bore Abraham a son in his old age, at the set time of which God had spoken to him. Even after Sarah displayed unbelief and laughed at the prophecy because in her mind she was stricken in age and it had ceased to be with her after the manner of women, even in this state of unbelief, God still visited Sarah, because He cannot lie.

There is also the account of the Shunemite woman as appears in **2 Kings 4:8–17.** The scriptures witness that when Elisha traveled to Shunem, the Shunemite woman *"constrained him to eat bread. And so it was, that as oft as he passed by, he turned in thither to eat bread."* Perceiving that Elisha was a holy man of God, the Shunemite woman impressed upon her husband that they should prepare a room for Elisha and set for him there a bed, and a table, and also a stool and a candlestick, so that when he visited them, he would stay there.

In the face of this hospitality, Elisha enquired through his servant Gehazi as to what could be done for the Shunemite woman:

*And he said, What then is to be done for her? And Gehazi answered, Verily she hath no child, and her husband is old. And he said, Call her. And when he had called her, she stood in the door. And he said, About this season, according to the time of life, thou shalt embrace a son. And she said, Nay, my lord, thou man of God, do not lie unto thine handmaid. And the woman conceived, and bare a son at that season that Elisha had said unto her, according to the time of life. (2 Kings 4:14–17)*

The Shunemite woman offered hospitality to the man of God, but had no expectation of any reward. She doubted the prophecy. Yet, in the midst of her unbelief the prophecy came to pass, because God: *"confirmeth the word of his servant and performeth the counsel of his messengers,"* Isaiah 44:26(a).

The giving and hospitality demonstrated by Sarah and the Shunemite woman provoked supernatural fruitfulness in their lives. The same happened to me as I testify.

Upon getting home from the church with the Winners' pastors, I immediately began rushing around getting lunch together. About five minutes later, Pastor Adams called my attention and asked me a very pertinent question: "Madam, where are your children?" I said to him, "I do not have any, sir." I then went on to explain the miscarriages. Pastor Adams told us that this was unscriptural. He asked my husband and I to stop everything we were doing and sit down. He asked us to open our Bibles to **Exodus 23:25–26**, which states: *"And ye shall serve the LORD your God, and he shall bless thy bread, and thy water; and I will take sickness away from the midst of thee. There shall nothing cast their young, nor be barren, in thy land: the number of thy days I will fulfil."*

This was the first time we came across this scripture or understood its importance. Pastor Adams explained to us, that insofar as we are serving God, nothing around us, including our dogs, chickens, etc., was permitted to suffer miscarriages or be barren. He asked us to key into the scripture in faith and see the hand of God. Thereafter, the pastors ate the lunch. Their entire stay in our residence was less than one hour.

Before they left, Pastor Adams asked us to join our hands with them in prayer. He prayed a very simple but heartfelt prayer. His prayer was to the effect that they had been persecuted in the land, and we were the first family to open our doors to them and feed them, without even knowing whom they were. Since the word of God says that whosoever receives a prophet in the name of a prophet shall receive a prophet's reward **(Matthew 10:41)**, he called on God to make our own prophet's reward the fruit of the womb. Thereafter, they collected our contacts and left.

My level of Christianity then did not enable me to understand the import of hospitality to men of God. So, I did not comprehend the spiritual implication of the visit until a few months later. I had sown seeds into the lives of the men of God and my reward was certain. As the Bible says: *"While the earth remaineth, seedtime and harvest, and cold and heat, and summer and winter, and day and night shall not cease," Genesis 8:22._*

## The Prophecy

Apparently, a few weeks after their visit to our residence, the two pastors were transferred from The Gambia to other countries by the Living Faith Church. Pastor Adams was transferred to Sierra Leone and Pastor Anzizi to Liberia. We were not aware of this fact because we had no further contact with the pastors after they left our residence.

On a certain day in February 1996, my husband and I returned from work and we received a strange telephone call. The call came from Pastor Adams, who was in Sierra Leone. My husband took the call in the bedroom, and then told me Pastor Adams wanted to talk to me. For you to understand how transient our contact with the pastors was, I had forgotten who Pastor Adams was. My husband had to refresh my memory.

When I picked up the phone, the pastor asked me, "Madam, are you pregnant?" I said no. He replied "God cannot lie. He spoke to me this morning concerning you." Pastor Adams explained that God told him that I would have a baby boy between October and November that year. He said that he had written a letter to this effect, which he anointed with oil and sent to us through ADC Airline, which used to fly to The Gambia weekly. However, the matter was so urgent it prompted him to make the telephone call. He instructed us to claim all the prophecies in the letter when we received it. Thereafter, he hung up.

I was stunned. I was on my monthly flow at that material point in time, wearing a sanitary towel. I just couldn't fathom the prophecy. The following day, the then-manager of the ADC Airline in The Gambia informed us that we had a letter from Sierra Leone. We collected the letter. It was a prophecy, repeating what Pastor Adams had told us on the phone. In the letter, he also stated that the only request he wanted to make was that the baby should be dedicated in Winners' Chapel. As instructed, my husband and I knelt down and claimed the prophecy.

## Fulfillment of Prophecy One

What happened to me next as I already captured above is similar to what happened to Sarah. I say this because two days after we received the prophecy I went to work hale and hearty with no sign of any ailment. About two hours after getting to work, I suddenly felt a chill descend on me. I was shivering and my temperature shot up. I had excruciating pains on the right side of my stomach and I could not stand up straight. I was immediately rushed to the Medical Research Council to meet my husband. Given the prophecy that had gone forth, my husband requested for a pregnancy test, which was done. The test came back negative.

The devil is a liar! The doctors then queried kidney stones because of the location of the pain. This necessitated that I should be taken to the Royal Victoria Hospital in Banjul to be attended by a specialist in that area. The doctor who attended to me at the hospital was one well known to us. He took the matter diligently. He scanned the kidneys and found nothing. He scanned the heart and found nothing. He then said, "Madam, I want to take a look at your womb."

My husband and I promptly informed him that we already ran a pregnancy test and besides, I was also on my monthly flow. The doctor said this was immaterial and insisted on scanning the womb. He spent the next forty-five minutes doing just that, after which he insisted that there was "something" in the womb measuring about three millimeters. He queried pregnancy and recommended that I should not be given any drugs likely to affect the pregnancy

Beloved, the pregnancy test was repeated one week later and it came back positive. A scan was done which showed a fetus in the womb, around six weeks old. I was six weeks pregnant and still having my menstrual flow. I had been pregnant four times prior to this, yet I did not perceive this pregnancy. My husband, who is a medical doctor and with whom I lived in the same house, did not see it, but the man of God all the way from Sierra Leone, another country, did. I was confounded, stunned, that a prophet in Sierra Leone could see my pregnancy in The Gambia. This was divine intervention. God had hidden the pregnancy away from the eyes of the devil and his agents. God moves in mysterious ways, His wonders to perform.

Let us not make any mistake about this: the days of the prophets are still here, the days of miracles are still here, the days of angelic interventions are still here. All it takes is the application of the right keys to command open heavens. In my case, it was simple: prayer and giving.

## Faith on the Wings of Signs and Wonders.

My faith began to grow on the wings of the prophecy and the wonders I was experiencing. As Jesus said to the nobleman in the book of John: *"Except ye see signs and wonders ye will not believe,"* John 4:48. My confidence that I was actually going to carry my own baby began to grow. My conviction was so much that when I began to bleed in the hospital, I was not afraid or anxious. Since I rejected fear, I did not open any door for the devil to steal the baby even though the devil tried very hard. I held unto my positive expectations.

My husband decided that I should return to Nigeria to have family care for me more effectively as his job was quite demanding then and he did quite a bit of travelling abroad. So, I went straight from the hospital where I was admitted to the airport and boarded a flight to Nigeria. My final destination was Enugu.

I began to bleed profusely during the journey. I was received at the airport by my older sister Dr. (Mrs.) Beatrice Onyeador, who was then resident in Enugu. She took me straight to a diagnostic laboratory to determine the viability of the baby because of the profuse bleeding. However, God had preserved the baby in spite of the bleeding and stress of the journey. I was eventually admitted in a hospital in Enugu, under the care of Dr. Iloabachie (deceased), who became like a father to me.

My sister took good care of me. She brought a nurse from her own private clinic to give extra help. My sister also cooked all my meals: breakfast, lunch and dinner. She never failed to do so. She was there 24/7. She did this despite the fact that she was also pregnant, was chronically hypertensive with the pregnancy, and had been admitted a couple of times in the hospital to curb the situation. She, however, put her own health and worries aside to take care of me. I remain eternally grateful to her. May the heavens continue to reward her labour of love.

Due to the fact that my mother was then away from Nigeria to the US, toward the end of my stay in the hospital my mother-in-law, Madam Patricia Awo Ota, took over my care in the hospital. She insisted on taking over from the nurse my sister had hired. Mama remained with me in the hospital until I was discharged. During this period, we fostered a bond. Consequently, I did not hesitate to relocate Mama to my home in the village upon its completion, where she had an uninterrupted and undisturbed possession of her own quarters for over twenty years and was well cared for until she passed on to glory. May her soul continue to rest in peace in the bosom of our Lord.

## Fulfillment of Prophecy Two and Three

When I was six months pregnant, my husband and I, who were still in shock due to the events leading up to the pregnancy, decided to ascertain the sex of the baby. This was to confirm whether the baby was a boy, as prophesied by Pastor Adams. *"O ye of little faith,"* **Matthew 8:26.**

I remember holding my breath during the scan. When the doctor said to me "It is a boy," I almost fainted thinking of the prophecy. I am awed at the greatness of God and the fulfillment of prophecy.

I returned to The Gambia when I was seven months pregnant in the company of my husband, who had travelled to Nigeria to pick me up. Our son, John Chukwuebuka Ota, was born on Sunday the thirteenth of October, 1996, delivered by the renowned Dr. Jack Faal, at Ndeban Clinic, Bakau. This was another fulfillment of prophecy. Pastor Adams had prophesied that the baby would be born between October and November 1996 and so it was. None of his words fell to the ground, as none of Samuel's words fell to the ground because God was with him: *"And Samuel grew and the Lord was with him and did let none of his words fall to the ground," 1 Samuel 3:19.*

## Fulfillment of Prophecy Four

Let me interpolate and observe here that, before I returned to The Gambia in August 1996, Winners' Chapel had been established in The Gambia and was holding services. Remember that the only request Pastor Adams made in the prophecy was for our baby to be dedicated in Winners' Chapel. My husband and I had wondered how that request was feasible because there were none of those churches in The Gambia.

God moves in mysterious ways, His wonders to perform. My husband told me that a few months after I left The Gambia, during my pregnancy, he received a phone call from a pastor in Sierra Leone, Pastor Dele Bamgboye, who introduced himself as one of the pastors of Winners' Chapel and the coordinator of Living Faith Churches in

West Africa. Apparently he had gotten our contact from either Pastor Adams or Pastor Azizi. Pastor Bamgboye informed my husband that two pastors from Winners' Chapel would be coming to The Gambia to establish a church and asked if my husband was available to receive them at the airport.

My husband jumped at the opportunity. So, on the appointed day and time, he proceeded to the airport and received the two pastors, namely Pastor Moses Oyedele and Pastor David Oladele-Darley.

Suffice it to say that upon my return back to The Gambia in August 1996, Winners' Chapel was holding services in The Gambia. In fact, there was a seminar ongoing in the church at the time John was born. Due to the testimony associated with his conception and birth, the pastors announced it right from the altar and the whole place exploded with cheers and dancing. Winners' members soon flooded the hospital to see the newborn baby.

As instructed by the man of God, John was dedicated in Winners' Chapel by Pastor Moses Oyedele and Pastor Anzizi, the same Pastor Anzizi who visited our house with Pastor Adams in 1995. What can't God do to perform the counsel of his messengers?

The arrival of Winners' Chapel in The Gambia at that time was divinely arranged to ensure the fulfillment of prophecy. This testimony has brought many into the kingdom. It is well documented in The Gambia and in every other country our family has been privileged to live in. Everyone congratulated us, including my mockers. Interestingly, some of my mockers brought me "pepper soup" and I ate it happily. They lost, I won. For: *"He disappointed the devices of the crafty, so that their hands cannot perform their enterprise," Job 5:12.*

John is currently twenty-four years old and is in the final stages of his training to become a medical doctor at the Kwame Nkrumah University of Science and Technology in Ghana. His Ibo name Chukwuebuka means "God is great." He is the epitome of humility, completely sold out to God and the interest of His kingdom. Upon his arrival in Ghana, he located a believing church where he fellowships.

We are not at all surprised by his interest in the things of God. We see it as fulfillment of prophecy.

As a teen, he was invited to preach in a few churches in The Gambia as a guest preacher during youth programs. He has a passion for lost souls, which engenders him to engage in active evangelism wherever he finds himself. He also uses his resources to ensure that the new converts are planted in the kingdom by hiring vehicles to convey them to church. A very kind soul, he can readily give up the last shirt on his back just to see someone smile. I cannot find enough words to describe John. He is indeed from above—a true child of prophecy and I know he will not disappoint destiny in Jesus' name.

*"When a prophet speaketh in the name of the Lord, if the thing follow not, nor come to pass, that is the thing which the Lord hath not spoken but the prophet hath spoken it presumptuously: thou shalt not be afraid of him," Deuteronomy 18:22.*

*John at ten months*

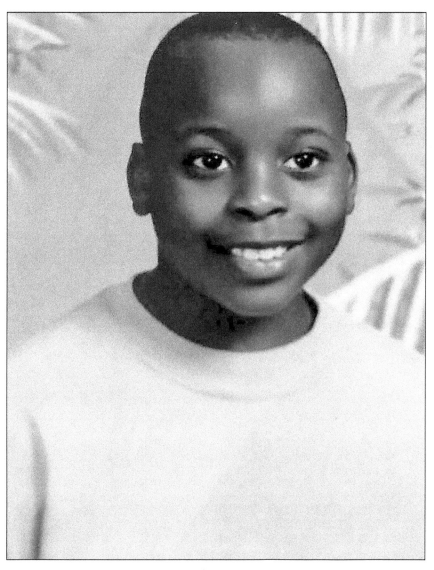

*John at nine years*

*John at twenty-one years*

# CHAPTER 5

# The Word of God

*For the word of God is quick and powerful, sharper than
any two-edged sword piercing even to the dividing asunder
of soul and spirit, and of the joints and marrow, and is a dis-
cerner of the thoughts and intents of the heart.*
**—Hebrews 4:12**

AS BISHOP OYEDEPO always says: "only fools doubt proofs." We had
seen the manifestation of the raw power of God in Winners' Chapel.
Therefore, our transition to Winners' Chapel was seamless. The testimony of the birth of our child is one that left no doubt in me that God
is real.

It is a testimony of: **"whereas I was blind, now I see," John 9:25,** an
undeniable miracle that planted us in the faith and in Winners' Chapel
for these twenty-four years. We soon settled down in the church.

However, exploits in the Kingdom of God do not depend on the
fact that you belong to a church noted for signs and wonders. Bishop
Oyedepo also always says, "God does not bless groups, He blesses
individuals."

Christianity is an individual race. It is a personal responsibility we
must undertake to access all the blessings of redemption. That is why
the Bible charges that we work out our own salvation with fear and
trembling **(Philippians 2:12).**

There is some work and labour involved and that work is in the word of God. It is pertinent that I digress a little at this juncture from the general gist of my testimony to emphasize the word of God and its potency. This will help us understand why I became a victim of the devil all over again even though I was an active member of a believing church. This is because I lacked the spiritual weapons contained in the word of God for supernatural exploits.

We must understand that the level of exploit that will command our inheritance in Christ depends on our level of spiritual development and commitment to the things of the kingdom, which are rooted in the word of God. According to scriptures, Jesus is the word of God and it is the light that He exudes through the word that shatters every darkness in our lives, giving us victory: *"In him was life; and the life was the light of men. And the light shineth in darkness; and the darkness comprehended it not," John 1:4-5.*

It is also pertinent to note that exploits in the kingdom are not obtained haphazardly. God is not the author of confusion. He is a God of order, as the Bible says: *"For God is not the author of confusion but of peace, as in all the churches of the saints," 1 Corinthians 14:33.*

So, in line with His program of orderliness, the Kingdom of God operates by keys that are domiciled in the word of God. For instance, if you give, then, you will receive i.e. fruitfulness as accounted by scriptures such as **Luke 6:38**. If you spread the gospel and win souls, God will decorate your life with goodness. This key is rooted firmly in several scriptures, such as **Romans 10:15**. The keys are legion. I have mentioned just a few.

It follows, therefore, that in the realm of the spirit the word of God is the only needful thing for exploits. As Jesus said to Martha when she complained that whilst she went about alone to cater to the material needs of Jesus, Mary sat at his feet to hear His word: *"Martha, Martha, thou art careful and troubled about many things. But one thing is needful and Mary hath chosen that good part, which shall not be taken away from her," Luke 10:41–42.*

Jesus was acknowledging the potency of the word of God as the only needful weapon that ensures a fulfilled life because God upholds all things by the word of His power **(Hebrews1:3)**.

This is the reality of the realm of the spirit. As a believer, rescued from the kingdom of darkness, you are to labour in the word of God to develop spiritual muscles for exploits. Therefore, Apostle Peter enjoins the believer, as newborn babes, to desire the sincere milk of the word, that you may grow thereby **(1 Peter 2:2)**.

This scripture suggests that the essence of the milk of the word is to ensure growth. This tells me that a believer is to grow beyond the milk level of the word. A grown man does not depend on milk for nourishment and strength again. To acquire strength, a grown man would eat solid food and strong meat. So it is also in the realm of the spirit. Maturity in the spirit realm requires a strong meat of the word. This is backed by the book of **Hebrews 5:13–14** as follows:

*"For every one that useth milk is unskillful in the word of righteousness; for he is a babe. But strong meat belongeth to them that are of full age, even those who by reason of use have their senses exercised to discern both good and evil."*

Accordingly, just as newborn babies drink milk for nourishment, strength, and growth, you as a believer are to eat the word of God for growth in spiritual strength, which qualifies you for exploits in the Kingdom. You are not to remain babies at the milk-drinking stage. Just as we eat food frequently—that is three square meals a day for nourishment—that is how a believer is to eat the word of God. By frequent study, meditation, and word practice, we acquire the strong meat of the word that makes for spiritual growth and fulfillment **(Jeremiah 15:16)**.

If, as a believer, even though a joint heir with Jesus by virtue of redemption, you refuse to grow in spiritual strength, choosing to remain a milk-drinking baby, you cannot be approved for kingship, which is entrance into your heritage of heaven right here on earth. Speaking about this position, the book of Galatians states:

*Now I say, That the heir, as long as he is a child, differeth nothing from a servant, though he be lord of all; But is under tutors and governors until the time appointed of the father. Even so we, when we were children, were in bondage under the elements of the world: But when the fullness of the time was come, God sent forth his Son, made of a woman, made under the law, to redeem them that were under the law, that we might receive the adoption of sons. And because ye are sons, God hath sent forth the Spirit of his Son into your hearts, crying, Abba, Father. Wherefore thou art no more a servant, but a son; and if a son, then an heir of God through Christ. (Galatians 4:1–7)*

So, the word builds up a believer from a baby to a son in the kingdom, then unto your heritage in Christ. Without the study, meditation, and practice of the word you cannot command the supernatural. That is the requirement for spiritual strength and capacity, to confront and dominate the kingdom of darkness in the days of adversity, so that you do not suffer shame and reproach.

## Why This Potency of the Word?

To my mind the word of God is so potent because it is the whole armour of God according to the book of Ephesians:

*Finally, my brethren, be strong in the Lord, and in the power of his might. Put on the whole armour of God, that ye may be able to stand against the wiles of the devil. For we wrestle not against flesh and blood, but against principalities, against powers, against the rulers of the darkness of this world, against spiritual wickedness in high places. Wherefore take unto you the whole armour of God, that ye may be able to withstand in the evil day, and having done all, to stand. Stand therefore, having your loins girt about with truth, and having on the breastplate of righteousness; And your feet shod with the preparation of the gospel of peace; Above all, taking the shield of faith, wherewith ye shall be able to quench all the fiery darts of the wicked. And take the helmet of salvation, and the sword of the Spirit, which is the word of God: Praying always with all prayer and supplication in the Spirit, and watching thereunto with all perseverance and supplication for all saints. (Ephesians 6:10-18)*

The Ephesians call the word an armour of God and the sword of the spirit. The word armour in this context is derived from the word armoury, which is defined by the Cambridge dictionary as follows:

(a) All the weapons and military equipment that a country owns; (b) A place where weapons and other military equipment are stored; (c) The metal coverings formerly worn to protect the body in battle; (d) Things or qualities that can be used to achieve a particular aim.

It follows that the word of God is the strong room where spiritual weapons, which we can employ to protect us in the days of battle, are kept. You must also understand that we are not in a physical but spiritual warfare. The Ephesians say, *"for we wrestle not flesh and blood."* The warfare is in the spirit realm. We are fighting spiritual forces such as principalities, powers, witches, and wizards, to mention but a few. These forces can only be surmounted with spiritual weapons. The fight is also evidently against our own earthly makeup, such as, our thoughts and imaginations that are contrary to the will of God. See **2 Corinthians 10:4–5.**

## What Are the Spiritual Weapons Contained in the Word of God?

**Ephesians 6:10–18,** which I captured above, showcases some of the vital spiritual weapons contained in the word of God as follows:

## 1. Righteousness

Righteousness is used interchangeably with holiness and godliness in scriptures. Without this vital key, no man can see God. This is because God's eyes are too pure to behold iniquity **(Habakkuk 1:13)**. Therefore, unrighteousness repels the presence of God and deprives us of access to our inheritance in Christ both here on earth and in eternity.

This is the truth as demonstrated in scriptures: ***"Know ye not that the unrighteous shall not inherit the kingdom of God? Be not deceived: neither fornicators nor idolators nor adulterers nor effeminate nor abusers of themselves with mankind nor thieves nor covetous nor drunkards nor revilers, nor extortioners, shall inherit the Kingdom of God," 1 Corinthians 6:9-10.***

What is salient is that it is the light/spirit in the word of God that sanctifies and enables the believer to live a life free of sins and iniquities. We should therefore hunger and thirst after righteousness via the word of God. This will empower our spiritual life into higher dimensions of supernatural exploits resulting in all-around rest, free from trouble.

See what Prophet Isaiah says about this: ***"And the work of righteousness shall be peace; and the effect of righteousness quietness and assurance forever. And my people shall dwell in a peaceable habitation, and in sure dwellings and in quiet resting places," Isaiah 32:17–18.***

## 2. Stewardship

This is the spirit of servanthood. It is service in the kingdom of God. A believer must actively engage in kingdom service by belonging to at least one service unit, such as sanctuary, choir, evangelism, ushering, prayer squad, etc. A believer must also pay tithes **(Malachi 3:10)** and offerings **(Psalms 96:8)**, as well as give to the less privileged **(Proverbs 19:17)**. The greatest service in the kingdom is, however, soul winning, which is God's heartbeat. It is for this that He sent His son Jesus to die on the cross to rescue mankind from destruction **(John 3:16)**. This is the only purpose for which Jesus came to the world. So, a believer must make salvation of souls and their preservation in the Kingdom a priority.

When we put God and the interest of His kingdom first by kingdom service, all the desires of our heart are granted. This is our assurance, according to the book of Matthew: ***"But seek ye first the kingdom of God, and his righteousness; and all these things shall be added unto you," Matthew 6:33.***

It follows that when we put the Kingdom of God first, we receive the desires of our heart. This is because of the rewards of stewardship, one of which is supernatural favour that grants speed and triggers signs and wonders. Esther had favour and she went from slavery to the throne **(Esther 2:17)**. Joseph was in prison but when the favour of God located him, he became a prime minister overnight **(Genesis 41:1-44)**. Mary had favour and she became the mother of Jesus **(Luke 1:30–33)**.

Stewardship also commands supernatural wisdom, which enthrones the believer in every sphere of life: **"And they that be wise shall shine as the brightness of the firmament; and they that turn many to righteousness as the stars forever and ever," Daniel 12:3.** The Bible also records that by wisdom, kings reign and princes decree justice, princes rule and nobles, even all the judges of the earth **(Proverbs 8:14–16)**.

### 3.  Prayer

As believers, we must pray for the outburst of revelations, which is the key to supernatural breakthroughs: ***"The eyes of your understanding being enlightened; that ye may know what is the hope of his calling, and what the riches of the glory of his inheritance in the saints," Ephesians 1:18.***

It is revelation that empowers us for exploits. Accordingly, a prayerless Christian is a powerless Christian. This is because

God reveals knowledge and understanding of Himself, His secrets, His plan and purpose for us, and divine direction in prayer. This is what is called revelation and it is accessed on the platform of prayer and fasting, which go hand in hand. Light breaks forth on the altar of prayer and fasting according to scriptures: *"Is not this the fast that I have chosen? To loose the bands of wickedness, to undo the heavy burdens, and to let the oppressed go free, and that ye break every yoke? Then shall thy light break forth as the morning, and thine health shall spring forth speedily, and thy righteousness shall go before thee, the glory of the Lord shall be thy rereward," Isaiah 58:6,8.*

The breaking forth of light is revelation. Without revelation, the believer cannot actualize destiny. For example, Jacob would not have accomplished his task without revelation. He was a complete nobody. His problem was his name and he had no knowledge of this. He laboured for years and had nothing to show for it. One day he apparently caught a better understanding and approached God in prayer. The Bible accounts that on Mount Peniel, Jacob was left alone and he wrestled with an angel until the breaking of day. He was labouring persistently, violently, and fervently in prayer. The fervency of his prayer was so much so that his hips dislocated. He refused to let go until God blessed him. God then changed his name from Jacob (which means supplanter, one who wrongfully or illegally seizes and holds the place of another) to Israel (which means triumphant with God). This is clear revelation, and from then onward, Jacob's destiny turned around for good **(Genesis 32:22–32)**.

There are also some demonic oppressions that cannot be delivered except on the grounds of prayer and fasting. An apt example is the case of the lunatic who was sore vexed with the devil. The disciples could not cast out the devil and Jesus said to them: *"Howbeit, this kind goeth not out but by prayer and fasting," Matthew 17:15–21.*

4. **Faith**

**Ephesians 6:16** says, *"Above all taking the shield of faith,"* a profound instruction that highlights how powerful the faith weapon is. This is because without faith, it is impossible to please God **(Hebrews 11:6)**. Life is to everyone according to his faith, because faith is the secret of the believer's strength. Consequently, God instructs us in four diverse scriptures, that the just shall live by faith **(Habakkuk 2:4, Romans 1:17, Galatians 3:11, Hebrews 10:38).**

This is not surprising because when a believer walks by faith he is simply telling God, "I believe you, I trust you, I trust your word, I have no other alternative, there is nothing else before you or after you." When a believer exhibits all these attributes of faith, it is pleasing to God and moves His hand to act, launching you into the supernatural. This is why **Matthew 17:20** says that if you have faith as small as a grain of mustard seed, you can move mountains and nothing shall be impossible unto you.

The Bible, testifying of the patriarchs of faith such as Gideon, Barak, Samson, Jephthae, David, Samuel, and the Prophets, declared: *"Who through faith subdued kingdoms, wrought righteousness, obtained promises, stopped the mouths of lions. Quenched the violence of fire, escaped the edge of the sword, out of weakness were made strong, waxed valiant in fight, turned to flight the armies of the aliens. Women received their dead raised to life again: and others were tortured, not accepting deliverance; that they might obtain a better resurrection," Hebrews 11:33–35.*

It is inexorably evident from the above scripture that faith destroys the siege of impossibilities, levels barriers, blusters confidence, accomplishes the impossible, and grants favour and speed. This shows that the beauty of our Christianity is rooted in faith, which commits God's integrity to carry out His word, no matter how precarious the terrain. We are overcomers in all circumstances, no matter the terrain.

However, faith cannot be obtained just for the asking. It is built up through personal responsibility of relentless study and meditation on the word of God. This is because faith comes by hearing, and hearing by the word of God **(Romans 10:17).** And having acquired faith you must put it to work. Take practical steps to manifest your faith in the physical, as faith without accompanying activities—practical steps demonstrating that faith—is unproductive, dead: *"What doth it profit my brethren, though a man say he hath faith and have no works? Can faith save him? For as the body without the spirit is dead, so faith without works is dead also," James 2:14,26.*

The woman with the issue of blood displayed the kind of faith with works that commanded open heavens. She had faith in her heart that merely touching the garment of Jesus would heal her. She took practical steps to actualize that healing. She fought through a mammoth crowd to get to Jesus. She persisted in the fight until she touched the hem of the garment of Jesus. What display of faith! To show you how potent her faith was, immediately after she touched Jesus' garment healing virtue left Him and located her and she received instant healing. Mind you, Jesus was in a crowd and I am sure a lot of people touched Him, but this woman's touch was mixed with faith and the heavens opened for her **(Mark 5:25-34).** Also, Abraham's faith was imputed to him for righteousness. He believed God that he was going to become the father of many nations. He did not weaken in faith even though his body was as good as dead, since he was about a hundred years old, and the womb of Sarah his wife was also dead. He demonstrated his faith by continuously giving glory to God **(Romans 4:18-22).** This moved God's hand to fulfill His promise.

5. **The Holy Spirit**

The Holy Spirit dwells inside the believer. He is God's presence in the life of the believer **(1Corinthians 3:16).** He quickens the believer by providing wise counsel to us, calling to our remembrance all the teachings in the word of God when we are faced with challenges. As the Bible says: *"But there is a spirit in man: and the inspiration of the Almighty giveth them understanding," Job 32:8.* That is why the Holy Spirit is called our helper **(John 14:26)**. He also helps the believer to live a righteous life by convicting us of our sins **(John 16:7–8)**. I have already stated that with righteousness in place, the believer attracts the presence of God, resulting in open heavens.

The Holy Spirit also guides the believer into all truths, including the knowledge of what is to come **(John 16:13–15)**. This attribute helps us not to fall into the trap of the devil and truncate our destiny. Additionally, the Holy Spirit triggers revelation. He opens our eyes to the riches of our glorious inheritance in Christ **(Ephesians 1:17–20).** I have already abundantly captured above that revelation is the key to supernatural breakthroughs.

Against this backdrop, believers should therefore demand for the manifestation of the Holy Spirit on the altar of prayer as He is the grand commander of signs and wonders. After Jesus returned in the power of the spirit, He began to command signs and wonders that even the winds obeyed Him **(Matthew 8 :23–27).** Furthermore, the disciples received power after the Holy Spirit came upon them, so that even the shadow of Peter became a healing tool as attested by the scripture below: *"Insomuch, that they brought forth the sick into the streets, and laid them on beds and couches, that at the least the shadow of Peter passing by might overshadow some of them. There came also a multitude out of the cities round about unto Jerusalem, bringing sick folks, and them which were vexed with unclean spirits; and they were healed every one," Acts 5:15-16.*

## My Empty Armoury

So, without adequate word base, a believer's life is empty, lacking in the requisite spirituality to confront the devil in the day of adversity. That was my situation after we became members of Winners' Chapel. I became very involved in many activities in the church. Although I was an active member of the sanctuary/sanitation unit, I was also involved in all weddings, naming ceremonies, and other social activities in the church. At some point I became the women's leader. My life was full of activities and noise.

In my limited understanding, this was the best way to show commitment in the church. In the midst of these activities, I lost sight of the only needful thing: the word of God. Do not get me wrong: as a member of a church you must belong to a service unit in the church and also participate in activities in the church. However, the priority must be the word of God. Even though I had gone to Word of Faith Bible Institute (WOFBI), run by Winners' Chapel, and acquired the Basic Certificate Course (BCC), I was not engaged in any active study or meditation on the word. Since I did not have the word, I lacked the requisite amour/weapons to confront the devil when he came knocking on my door again.

We must be sensitive to the fact that life is a continuous spiritual battle against the devil. Once you are a believer, you are a candidate for the temptation of the devil because his greatest nightmare is when a soul is rescued from the kingdom of darkness. If he even tempted Jesus the son of God **(Matthew 4:1–11),** then who are we? That is why Apostle Peter admonishes believers to be sober and vigilant, because our adversary the devil, as a roaring lion, is going about looking for who to destroy **(1 Peter 5:8–9).** Our vigilance stems from our knowledge of the word of God.

Accordingly, the devil is a remorseless tempter. Though he may leave us for a season, he always returns and if he finds us empty of the word, empty of faith, and lacking in spiritual strength, he attacks with greater torments. This is a fact depicted in scriptures as follows:

*When the unclean spirit is gone out of a man, he walketh*
*through dry places, seeking rest, and findeth none. Then he*
*saith, I will return into my house from whence I came out;*
*and when he is come, he findeth it empty, swept, and gar-*
*nished. Then goeth he, and taketh with himself seven other*
*spirits more wicked than himself, and they enter in and dwell*
*there: and the last state of that man is worse than the first.*
*Even so shall it be also unto this wicked generation. (Matthew*
*12:43–45)*

I was in this state of spiritual emptiness when I got pregnant again in 1998. I was elated, especially when I discovered that I was carrying a set of twins, two boys. I had delivered John in 1996, on the wings of angels and prophets, so what could possibly go wrong?

I did not realize that every case is different, every battle different, with different strategies requiring a host of diverse spiritual weapons. So, I took very few steps to empower myself spiritually through the knowledge of the word of God. I was to pay a very high price for this ignorance and lack of knowledge.

I began to make elaborate plans to travel to the US to deliver the boys and also take advantage of the care of my mother, who was then in the US. I fixed my travel date for Sunday 20 September 1998. On Friday 18 September 1998, at around 5:00 p.m., whilst I was packing up John's things (he was to travel to the US with me), my "water" broke and I went into premature labour.

The pregnancy was then barely five months old. I was rushed to the same hospital where John was delivered, and was promptly attended to by the same doctor who delivered John. The doctor did everything humanly and medically possible to stop the labour, but to no avail. The boys were born prematurely.

In those days, The Gambia lacked adequate medical parameters to sustain babies of such extreme prematurity. Consequently, after struggling to keep them alive, the boys died within fifteen minutes of each other.

Thus, I lost to the devil. I was like a soldier at the warfront without any armour to combat a very insidious enemy. I had no word base. I could not tell the devil "it is written" as Jesus did, because I had no knowledge of anything written in the book. I had no faith at all; rather, I was crying like a defeated soldier. The little light I had in me had gone out and darkness had come back. All in all, I had no spiritual strength for the battle. Therefore, I was vanquished. As the Bible says: *"If thou faint in the day of adversity, thy strength is small," Proverbs 24:10.* Indeed, my strength was small.

I was devastated, inconsolable. I lost sense of the times and seasons. I lost sight of John, my husband, my job, home, and friends. I also had to deal with all the physical issues associated with an after birth without any baby to show for it. So, I retreated completely into myself. My mental health was affected, another torment of the devil. I began to hallucinate about the boys. I saw them everywhere. I heard them crying everywhere. The devil is indeed a ruthless enemy, particularly when he finds an ignorant victim.

On the request of family in Nigeria, my husband sent John and I back to Nigeria. This time around I went to my elder sister, Mrs. Florence Chinedu Ononiwu in Abuja. She is the prayer warrior of the family. I stayed about two months with her, during which time she never gave up on me or in God's ability to intervene in my situation. She took leave of absence without pay from her employers so she could nurse me back to health. She prayed fervently without ceasing, morning, afternoon and night. God answered.

I recovered physically and mentally and eventually returned to The Gambia. I remain eternally grateful to my sister Mrs. Florence Chinedu Ononiwu. God used her mightily in my healing process. May the Almighty God continue to bless you in Jesus' name.

Upon my return to The Gambia, I continued to fellowship at Winners' Chapel, but I had completely lost any little faith I had in God. I was living in torment. Given that I was not allowed to see the boys and was never told where they were buried, thoughts of them consumed me.

The devil seized my mind and fueled my imagination with very negative thoughts. When it rained, I would stand by the window and cry, imagining the rain falling on the boys. If it was too hot, I would imagine how uncomfortable the boys felt in the heat.

Even though I went to church regularly, I was merely going through the motions, because my mind was elsewhere. I lived in perpetual fear of the unknown.

I got pregnant five more times and lost all of them. None of those pregnancies progressed beyond two months. In fact, some were lost at less than six weeks. The devil and his host of demons had turned me into their favourite playground. By count, I lost a total of ten pregnancies to the devil, four before the birth of John and six after his birth. This is ten pregnancies and eleven babies, counting the twins as two babies. The tenth pregnancy was lost in the US where I moved to live with my family in 2002. Certainly not a good testimony. I however refused to give up because: *"a just man falleth seven times and riseth up again," Proverbs 24:16.*

# Enough Is Enough

*And when the Angel stretched out his hand upon Jerusalem*
*to destroy it,*
*the Lord repented him of the evil, and said to the Angel that*
*destroyed the people,*
*it is enough: stay now thine hand.*
**—2 Samuel 24:16**

IN 2002 MY husband got an appointment to work at the Johns Hopkins University School of Public Health, in Maryland, US. This necessitated that our family move from The Gambia to live in the US. I had never wanted to live in the US, which I always saw as a vacation resort. However, since the job came with a degree of status, in that we were all given social security cards before leaving The Gambia, I agreed to relocate. Shortly before leaving for the US, I discovered I was pregnant again. Given the stress of packing up to leave and the journey itself, I lost the pregnancy shortly after I arrived in the US. That was the tenth miscarriage.

I was too busy to mourn this particular loss due to the challenges of settling down in the US, especially with the schooling of John, who was then six years old. John had missed a full term of the American school session and I spent a lot of time homeschooling him to bring him up to speed. This initial activity kept me quite busy. However, after John started school fully, I had a lot of time on my hands.

Living in America to me was completely different than vacationing there. Usually during my vacations, my host would create time to take me to some recreational activities. Living in America was a different ball game. I had no hosts, no friends initially, and no family members near me. My sister, Dr. Beatrice Onyeador, who had relocated to the US, lived in New Jersey and so did my brother. I could only talk to both on phone. Even though immediately upon arrival in the US we sought out a believing church in our neighbourhood, Restoring Life International Church, and began to fellowship there, I was not really involved in social activities in the church. Not getting overly involved in social activities in the church was a deliberate choice I had made. I had taken stock of my spiritual growth and found it sadly lacking. I had made up my mind to build up my spiritual strength.

We had taken a lot of spiritual materials from Winners' Chapel, The Gambia, to the US. This included books of the ministry authored by Bishop David Oyedepo and Pastor Faith Oyedepo, anointing oil, mantles, our church notebooks, and spiritual tapes. So, in my state of isolation, I began a study I had never done before. I began rereading all the bishop's books, such as *Satan Get Lost, Born to Win,* and a host of others. I listened to messages by the bishop. I studied the notes I had taken in Winners' Chapel, The Gambia, from my church notebooks, an activity I had never done before. I also studied the Bible alongside all these other spiritual materials, and slowly light began to seep into my Spirit: ***"The light of the body is the eye: if therefore thine eye be single thy whole body shall be full of light,"*** *Matthew* ***6:22.***

Forever the scriptures cannot be broken. Consequently, with the entrance of the word, light came, and with light, I began to gain understanding on how to handle the devil. I found that the devil is not a lion that could not be defeated, but is like a roaring lion. He is not the real thing but a poor imitation of a lion. He can easily be defeated by the correct application of the right word in faith. All the word study blustered and strengthened my faith. The devil was soon to temp this newly acquired faith.

In early 2003, just after a few months of stay in the US and for no apparent reason, I began to bleed heavily. I was not pregnant. I was not on my monthly flow, but the blood kept coming, requiring that I wear sanitary towels every day. We were confounded. Given that my husband was working at the Johns Hopkins establishment we decided to book an appointment to have a medical checkup.

Now, Johns Hopkins hospital is known as the Center of Excellence. It is rated as one of the best hospitals in the world. When the hospital gives you a diagnosis, according to science, it is about 99 percent precise. So, the word of the hospital in the field of science was law and could not be gainsaid.

Fortunately, I had a different mentality. On the appointed date, I went with my husband to the hospital. They ran some quick tests, and did extensive scans, some of which I had never done before. Thereafter, they came up with an immediate prognosis. They informed us that my womb had been overtaken by fibroids. These fibroids were the cause of my miscarriages. The fibroids were so big that no baby could ever survive in my womb. Due to the size and the number of fibroids, a surgery to remove them was not an option. The only solution was to do a hysterectomy, which is a surgery to remove the womb completely. If not, I would continue bleeding, which could be fatal.

In effect the hospital told me that I should not bother with thoughts of more babies, because I could not have any. Due to the fact that we had a better understanding, we rejected the verdict and refused to be scheduled for a hysterectomy. The hospital told us to take three months to think about this and if we changed our minds we could schedule an appointment for a review. We refused to accept even this option.

Bishop Oyedepo always says, "Whatever you don't want, you don't watch, whatever you don't resist is permitted to remain and whatever you don't confront you don't conquer."

It was time for me to confront the devil. It was time for me to say to the wicked one, "Enough is enough." So, I began an aggressive study of the word on healing. I told myself that Jesus bore my cross to Calvary,

He bore my griefs and sorrows, was smitten, stricken, and afflicted. He was wounded for my transgressions, bruised for my iniquities, and by His stripes my healing was secured years ago **(Isaiah 53:4–5)**. He himself took my infirmities and bore my sicknesses **(Matthew 8:17)**, therefore, I cannot be sick. I cannot have fibroids because when Jesus cried, "It is finished!" on the cross, everything negative in my life, including these demonic fibroids, were finished.

I reminded God of how Jesus had healed the woman who had the issue of blood for twelve years. I called on God to see my faith and also heal me. I reminded God of countless testimonies of healing in Winners' Chapel, including fibroids that turned to babies. I called on God to turn my fibroids into babies. There is power in positive declarations. This is why the scriptures say that life and death are in the power of the tongue (**Proverbs 18:20–21**).

Therefore, what you say about yourself determines the outcome of any situation. This is because our words are the products of our thoughts. Since the mind is the womb of expectations, it follows that what we speak is what we expect to see, and whatever we expect is what we get *"for surely there is an end, and thine expectation shall not be cut off," Proverbs 23:18*.

Forever God's word is settled in heaven. Accordingly, if you speak life into any dead situation it will rise again. Just see the account of the valley of dry bones in the book of **Ezekiel 37**. This was a dead situation, an impossible situation, a valley full of bones. The Bible says the bones were very dry. Not only were these bones in a valley, a pit, the grave, representing captivity, they were also very dry, lifeless. When positive words were spoken, they came back to life.

The same book of Ezekiel also states that after the bones came back to life, the word of God went to open up the graves so that the people of Israel came out of their graves (trials, captivity) and entered into their inheritance. That is the power of positive declarations.

It is also pertinent to know here that as believers we are always surrounded by angels. They are our ministering spirits *(***Hebrews 1:13–14***)*. They are always there to do our bidding. When we speak they take our words directly to God for performance. They are like robots. They do not filter or rationalize anything you say. If you say positive things about any situation, they carry the words verbatim to God for performance. If you also say negative things, they carry them verbatim to God as your expectation. So you have to be careful what you say about any situation, because you cannot take back your words as an error once they are spoken. Consequently, the Bible admonishes: *"Suffer not thy mouth to cause thy flesh to sin; neither say thou before the Angel, that it was an error: wherefore should God be angry at thy voice, and destroy the work of thine hands?"* **Ecclesiastes 5:6.**

## Great Faith

Thus, positive words rooted in scriptures make dead situations live again. Such was my case, as I continued to express my faith by confessing positive scripture-loaded words. About two months after I was given the verdict requiring me to undergo surgery to remove my womb, I suddenly fell ill. I had all the signs of early pregnancy. I bought a home pregnancy kit from a nearby pharmacy and conducted a pregnancy test, which was positive. Thereafter, I booked an appointment to see the doctors at the hospital. They were skeptical. They told me that the pregnancy would not progress beyond three months because of the fibroids. They recommended that I go through with the hysterectomy to remove the womb and the fetus together. I refused and chose to keep the pregnancy.

It was a spiritual battle and I felt that I had a more potent weapon: my faith demonstrated by the bold declaration of the word of God. Since I had no other medical alternatives other than the hysterectomy, as no drug could be administered to save the situation, I had only one focus: God. When you have no other alternatives than God, He steps in and takes over your battle.

Therefore, God stepped in and took over my battle. The pregnancy progressed beyond the three months but the devil did not give up easily. At about four months he struck again. I suddenly began to feel more sick than normal. Even though I was still bleeding and wearing sanitary towels daily (I bled and wore sanitary towels all through the pregnancy), I had however at this stage gotten over the sickness, nausea, and lethargy usually associated with the first trimester of pregnancy.

So when I began to be sick again at four months, especially after meals, I knew there was something not right with my system. I booked an appointment to see the doctors at the hospital. They were very surprised that the pregnancy had advanced beyond their predicted three months. They conducted a blood sugar test and identified that it was unusually high. Accordingly, I had developed what is called gestational diabetes, which is diabetes triggered off by pregnancy.

The hospital declared the pregnancy high-risk. I was given two options to curb the diabetes: either to take medication (insulin) or go on a strict diet. I immediately rejected the medication and opted for the diet even in the midst of the pregnancy. It is the desperate faith of men that commands open heavens. I was desperate not to allow anything, including medication, to terminate the pregnancy. Therefore, I began to exercise very great faith. Consequently, I was sent to the nutritional clinic of the hospital, where a strict diet was prescribed for me to follow.

Pregnancies are associated with a lot of eating, both for the health of the baby and the mother. But in my situation the reverse was the case. The diet was gruesome. It consisted of one slice of toast and half a glass of sugar-free juice for breakfast. For lunch, I took half a cup of boiled rice, one half of a chicken thigh, half of an apple, and water. For dinner, I had half a soup bowl of custard or oatmeal. I had a test kit and a chart to enter my blood sugar level after every meal. This entailed pricking my fingers to obtain blood samples for the test three times daily. I was determined to win this battle, so I took the diet and blood sugar tests with the same discipline with which I had learned to approach my spiritual life. God intervened and the sugar level stabilized. I, however, continued with the diet and blood test on doctor's recommendation to avoid a spiking of the sugar level again.

One would think that at this stage, the devil would give up, but no. He is an unrepentant adversary. He showed up again when the pregnancy turned five months. From the time I discovered that I was pregnant, I had a conviction that the baby was a boy. I confirmed this at three months. Since we had named our children when we came in contact with Winners' Chapel, I knew that this baby was David, named after our beloved Prophet, Bishop David Oyedepo. I spoke to the baby every day, calling him by his name and prophesying over his life.

At five months my baby bump was quite visible and was a constant attraction for John, who was then seven years old. I had told him that it was his brother David in the abdomen. John was very excited and curious to know how his brother looked like. As a result of this, at five months when I felt the fetus should be well developed, I decided to take John to the hospital with me on one of my routine antenatal checkups. This was to enable him see the fetus, his brother, when being scanned, a process I had to undergo during my antenatal sessions.

When the scanning began, I initially did not perceive any problem as John was very excited seeing the baby on the monitor. A few minutes into the scanning, the doctor paused and made a call, and two other doctors joined him. They were to make subsequent calls and I soon had a lot of doctors in the room all reviewing the images on the monitor and conferring in very sophisticated medical terms.

Subsequently, the doctors called my husband from his office to join us at the antenatal clinic. When my husband arrived, the doctors told us that the baby in my womb had multiple abnormalities. These abnormalities would make it impossible for him to survive till full-term of pregnancy. If he did somehow survive through the pregnancy, he would suffer and still die in early infancy.

The abnormalities mentioned included: a small head (microcephaly), very short legs and arms, a blocked esophagus (esophageal atresia), and a very small stomach, to mention but a few. They explained that should the baby survive until his delivery a tube would have to be passed through a hole made on his abdomen to his stomach for feeding since nothing could pass through his esophagus, thereby making normal feeding through the mouth impossible. They also said that it would be impossible for him to walk all his life as the size of his brain and limbs could not support a normal life. In view of their supposed abnormalities, they suggested that the pregnancy be terminated at this stage, as it was not worth the effort and suffering carrying it further.

Recall that John was in that room and had been paying rapt attention to the ongoing discussion. He began to cry, asking why the doctors were saying his brother was sick—an experience he still remembers to this day. My husband rose up in holy anger and declared, "It is not possible; His gifts are without repentance, there is absolutely nothing wrong with the baby." He asked me to get up and let us go home. The doctors tried to convince us, appealing to his medical and scientific senses. My husband was to tell me a few years later that he could see what the doctors were talking about from the images on the scan but he refused to confess it or accept it. So we rejected the report, refused to terminate the pregnancy as recommended, and went home.

## The Mysteries

Since the battle had gotten hotter, we decided to adopt a more radical approach by employing all the mysteries of the kingdom. These are also our weapons of warfare, as identified in the word of God. To some these mysteries are incomprehensible, but God enlightens the understanding of His children. As Jesus declared: *"Unto you it is given to know the mysteries of the Kingdom of God: but to others in parables; that seeing they might not see, and hearing they might not understand," Luke 8:10*.

I will endeavour to capture these mysteries and some of their attributes briefly below, according to my understanding, as inspired by the Holy Spirit and the instructions I received from my Prophet and pastors through the years. My prayer is that the Holy Spirit grants everyone understanding in Jesus' name, Amen.

### 1. The Holy Anointing Oil

One of these weapons is the mystery of the anointing oil. We first see this in the book of **Exodus 30:22-31**. In that scripture, God commanded Moses to anoint the tabernacle of the congregation, the ark of testimony, the table and all the vessels, the candlestick and his vessel, the altar of incense, the altar of burnt offering with all his vessels, the laver, and Aaron and his sons with the holy anointing oil. This is so that they would be most holy, and whatsoever touched them should be holy. We are instructed to do this for all the generations to come. Therefore, using the anointing oil in these modern times is commanded by scriptures.

One may wonder: what is the anointing oil? From the scriptures cited above, we see that one of the components of the anointing oil is just olive oil, which can be purchased from the store. When it is prayed over and declared in faith to be the anointing oil, the Holy Spirit sanctifies it and makes it holy.

Holiness attracts God's presence in our lives, which breaks down barriers and works outstanding miracles. When the children of Israel left Egypt, they carried the presence of God. Consequently, they overcame every challenge in their way. The sea saw the presence of God and fled, Jordan was driven back, the mountains skipped like rams and the hills like lambs, the rock was turned into a standing water and the flint into a fountain of waters, and the whole earth trembled **(Psalms 114:1–8).**

Additionally, the Holy Spirit in the anointing oil is the grand commander of signs and wonders. He provokes instant supernatural intervention, breaks all yokes including sicknesses, diseases, curses, spells, and enchantments, leading to breakthroughs. This is clear from **Isaiah 10:27: *"And it shall come to pass in that day, that his burden shall be taken away*** *from off thy shoulder, and his yoke from off thy neck, and the yoke shall be destroyed because of the anointing."*

The healing power of the Anointing oil is further emphasized by **James 5:14–15** in the following words: *"Is any sick among you? Let him call for the elders of the church, and let them pray over him anointing him with oil in the name of the Lord. And the prayer of faith shall heal the sick, and the Lord shall raise him up."* Equally, in **Mark 6:13,** when Jesus sent the disciples out to preach the gospel, the Bible accounts *"and they cast out devils, and anointed with oil many that were sick, and healed them."*

The healing and yoke-breaking power of the anointing oil cannot therefore be gainsaid. Armed with this knowledge and with faith and spiritual understanding that underscore delivery of our inheritance in Christ, I began an aggressive adventure with the mystery of the anointing oil, one that has remained with our family until this day. My husband and I got out all the anointing oil we took to the US from Winners' Chapel, The Gambia. I drank a shot of the anointing oil and anointed my stomach every day, declaring every sickness and yoke of the devil upon my baby and I, broken, in Jesus' name.

## 2. The Holy Communion

The mystery of the Holy Communion was first administered by Jesus to His disciples. This is also known as the Lord's Supper. The book of **Matthew 26:26–28** evidences that this was the last meal Jesus had with His disciples before His crucifixion. At supper, Jesus gave bread and wine to His disciples representing His body and blood; this is known as the Holy Communion. These were symbols of His new covenant. He further charged His disciples to do this often, in remembrance of Him. This means that Christians are to take the Communion often, in remembrance of Jesus (**1 Corinthians 11:24–26).**

The Bible tells us that Jesus bore our griefs, carried our sorrows, was wounded for our transgressions, bruised for our iniquities, the chastisement of our peace was upon him, and by His stripes we were healed **(Isaiah 53:3–4)**. So, there is healing virtue in the body and blood of Jesus which is part of our redemptive package. That is why the book of **Leviticus 17:11** declares that the life of the flesh is in the blood. The book of **Revelation 12:11** also shows that we overcome all, including, all the trials of life, principalities, powers, the forces of darkness, all the wiles of the devil, sicknesses, and diseases by the blood of the Lamb (Jesus) and by the word of our testimony.

Speaking about the potency of the Communion in giving the believer immunity over all manners of sicknesses and diseases as well as mastery over all facets of life, in the book titled *The Power of the Communion Table*, Pastor (Mrs.) Faith Oyedepo declared in **pages 6–8**:

> *The apostles, who left a mark on the sands of time, did not take the Communion lightly; they were so particular about it that they broke bread daily, both in the temple and from house to house. This is made abundantly clear in (Acts 2:46). The Communion Table- The Lord's Supper, is a new testament mystery designed by God to give the believer unhindered access to frequent mastery, in every area of life. The Communion is a mystery meal that restores our body and gives us life that is immune to all sicknesses and diseases.*

I therefore began to take the Communion every day in faith, believing in God for the perfection of my health and that of the baby in my womb. I would pray over every food and drink, declaring them to be the body and blood of Jesus before taking them. My family has continued to take the

Communion every day; we administer the Communion on our prayer altar daily.

### 3. The Blood of Sprinkling

The mystery of the Blood of Sprinkling emanates from the book of **Exodus chapters 11 and 12**, where God delivered the people of Israel from Egypt with a strong arm. After all the plagues that God sent to the Egyptians failed to engender Pharoah, the king of Egypt, to let the children of Israel go, God delivered His last card, the blood of sprinkling. God instructed Moses to tell the children of Israel to kill a lamb for each household, take of the blood, and strike it on the two side posts and on the upper door post of the houses wherein they eat it. God would pass through the land of Egypt that night and smite all the firstborn in the land of Egypt, both man and beast, and against all the gods of Egypt He would execute judgment. When He saw the blood He would pass over the Israelites, and would not smite them.

The purpose of the blood of sprinkling as can be extrapolated from the scriptures above is that it exempts us from the evils in the world. It is our stronghold against principalities and powers and all the forces of darkness. In the order of the new covenant, we no longer employ the blood of lambs or any animal for the mystery of the blood of sprinkling. This is because we have a higher order, which is the blood of Jesus, who is our Passover lamb (**1 Corinthians 5:7).**

Since Jesus remains our Passover lamb, all one has to do to actualize this mystery is to pour some water in a bowl and pray over it, declaring it in faith to be the blood of Jesus the Passover lamb. This is exactly what I did. Then I would sprinkle the blood over myself and all inhabitants of my home, on the doorposts inside and outside the house, declaring our exemption from all the plagues of Egypt, including death, sicknesses, and diseases.

It is important to note that engaging in the mystery of the blood of sprinkling in this day and age is scriptural. The Bible tells us to observe this mystery forever: **"And ye shall observe this thing for an ordinance to thee and to thy sons forever,"** **Exodus 12:24.**

### 4. Feet Washing

This mystery was introduced to us in the book of **John 13:5-10**, where Jesus washed the feet of His disciples. As the scripture attests, by feet-washing we become a part of Jesus. This means that when our feet are washed in the name of Jesus, if we have faith and understanding in our hearts, we access every part of Jesus: His power, riches, wisdom, strength, honour, glory, and blessings. These are all the attributes deposited in Jesus according to **Revelation 5:12**, which states *"Saying with a loud voice, Worthy is the Lamb that was slain to receive power, and riches, and wisdom, and strength, and honour, and glory, and blessing."*

The strength signifies physical, spiritual, and mental strength. These connote all round health free from sickness and disease. Feet washing translates us into the realm of the supernatural, empowering us to tread upon serpents and scorpions and over all the powers of the enemy and nothing shall by any means hurt us **(Luke 10:19).**

### 5. The Mantle

God is the moderator of the transference of the spirit of a prophet to his faithful followers. These are believers who receive the person of the prophet, believe in him and his ministry, desire the blessings and grace of God upon him, honour him, and faithfully follow him. A believer who is completely connected to a prophet in such a dimension receives a flow of the grace he carries. One of the mediums for this flow of grace or transference of spirit, is the mantle. This is any clothing material taken from the body or hands of the prophet, for example, handkerchiefs, cloaks, scarfs, aprons, to mention but a few. This is because the grace upon a prophet flows to whatever touches him.

We see this transference of spirit or grace from Prophet Elijah to his faithful servant Prophet Elisha in **2 Kings 2:1–15.** This account shows the sort of unrelenting belief and followership of a prophet that earns the transference of the grace that the prophet carries to the believer. Elisha refused to give up on Elijah, who was to be taken up to heaven on that day, even in the face of mockery and discouragement by the other sons of the prophets. Therefore, he procured the grace and anointing upon Elijah via Elijah's cloak (mantle) and began to perform instant miracles. His mockers, the sons of the prophets, bowed down to him thereafter. Elisha became one of the greatest prophets in Israel, greater than Elijah because he had a double portion of the anointing upon Elijah.

The anointing was still at work years after Elisha had been dead and buried. The Bible records that when a dead person was thrown into the grave of Elisha, and the body touched the bones of Elisha, that the dead man came back to life and stood on his feet **(2 Kings 13:21).**

The mantle is thus for healing and destruction of the forces of darkness. This is also seen in the ministry of Apostle Paul, as accounted in the Acts of the Apostles, where handkerchiefs and aprons that had come in contact with the body of Apostle Paul became mediums of healing and the destruction of evil spirits **(Acts 19:11–12).**

There is also the testimony of the woman with the issue of blood, who believed that merely touching Jesus' garment would make her well. So, she proceeded to touch Jesus' garment in faith and received instant healing. The healing virtue in Jesus was available in his garment for anyone that would touch it with faith **(Mark 5:24–34).**

We had taken our mantles from Winners' Chapel, The Gambia to the US. These mantles are handkerchiefs that had come in contact with the body of Prophet Bishop Oyedepo, who has never been sick for over fifty years. I coveted this perfect health. I always had a mantle on my body, usually around my neck or my arm, believing in God for my healing and that of my baby as well as the destruction of every work of darkness in my life.

CHAPTER **7**

# My Double Rewards

*For your shame ye shall have double;*
*and for confusion they shall rejoice in their portion;*
*therefore, in their land they shall possess the double;*
*everlasting joy shall be unto them.*
**—Isaiah 61:7**

## King David

I CONTINUED TO pray, study the word of God, administer all the mysteries of the Kingdom, and make positive declarations with faith. At thirty-seven weeks of pregnancy, on the sixth of January 2004, a very cold and blistering day in Baltimore, Maryland, I proceeded to the hospital in the morning for a routine antenatal care visit. After the doctor scanned the baby, I was told that the baby was stressed in the womb. He was losing weight instead of gaining, so the doctor wanted the baby out that day. He suggested that the surest way was by cesarean section due to the delicate nature of the pregnancy, since the baby may not survive the stress associated with normal labour and delivery. I refused the cesarean section, insisting on a normal delivery. Consequently, they induced labour. Given that they had suspected multiple abnormalities I had a number of specialist doctors in the delivery room with me at the time of his delivery.

71

David Inya-Ama Chikadibia Ota was born on the sixth of January 2004 at 6:24 p.m. He weighed four pounds seven ounces. He was so little that clothes meant for premature babies were too big for him. Immediately after birth, and because they expected an abnormal baby, David was taken away to the intensive care unit where very sick babies are looked after.

About two hours later, two nurses came from the intensive care unit and told me that David had been taken from the intensive care unit to the nursery, where normal newborns are kept. They said that he was crying so much at the top of his voice that he was disturbing the other very sick babies in the intensive care unit and making them cry along. I said to them "Praise the Lord" because I knew there was nothing wrong with David. He was only looking for me.

I told them to take me to the nursery to see him so that he could be pacified. They obliged. When we got to the nursery, I found David inside an incubator and wailing at the top of his voice. I put my hands into the incubator to touch him. I called his name and he immediately kept quiet. I asked that he be brought out of the incubator and placed on my chest, which they did. He immediately fell asleep on my chest. That became the order of our stay in the hospital.

I was discharged forty-eight hours after birth since I was perfectly healthy and normal. David was however left behind in the hospital as the doctors wanted him to attain the weight of five pounds and be certified fit before his discharge. This meant that I had to go home without my baby, which was very traumatizing. I was, however, in the hospital every day, from 7:00 a.m. until 10:00 p.m. at night when I was required to vacate the nursery. Apparently, David had gotten used to my voice while in the womb from my consistent prayers and confessions over his life. Thus, he would cry most of the night when I left him to go home and keep quiet as soon as I arrived in the morning and took him out of the incubator.

Consequently, I had an unwritten understanding with the medical personnel in the nursery. They would give David to my care as soon as I arrived at the nursery and leave him in my care until I left. I never faulted in the care of my baby, even though it was very stressful considering that I also needed care having just given birth. Due to the stress and lack of care, I developed oedema (swelling in the ankles, feet, and legs) and my episiotomy (an incision made from my private part to my anus to give David an easier passage during delivery) got infected and broke down completely. This caused me excruciating pain but did not deter me from caring for my baby. On the eighth day after birth we insisted on circumcising David as instructed by scriptures **(Genesis 17:10–14)** and the hospital obliged after much debate.

About two weeks after his birth I found a team of doctors waiting for me on my arrival in the morning. They had also sent for my husband, who arrived at the nursery afterward. The doctors apologized to us, saying they had run a lot of tests on David and found none of the abnormalities that they thought he had during pregnancy. They said they were confused and could not understand what had happened. They also said that they had seen my dedication to the care of the baby since his admission to the nursery. Therefore, even though that David had not attained the five-pound weight desired, they were confident to discharge him to our care at home because they believed he would thrive better at home.

I was overjoyed that there were no abnormalities. I knew that the Almighty God, the King of Kings, the Creator of the whole world, Jehovah Rapheka our healer, brought His spare parts from heaven and replaced all the ones the doctors detected to be broken down. He gave David a brand-new neck, head, stomach, lungs, limbs, throat, and made him perfectly whole. I give God all the glory.

David, whom the doctors said would be so abnormal that he would never be able to walk all his life if he survived, walked at nine months to the glory of God. He is a very intelligent, ingenious, spirit-filled, and handsome young man who the devil wanted to steal from us if we had allowed him. At the time of this publication, David is sixteen years old and just started the International Baccalaureate 2 (IB 2) at the International School of Brussels, Belgium. He has plans of proceeding to Canada next year to pursue his tertiary education in the field of architecture. A very loving soul and a dedicated steward in the kingdom. At the young age of fourteen he joined the Ushering Unit of Winners' Chapel, Brussels, where he has proved himself. He also engages actively in prayer and fasting whenever the need arises. I know he will fulfill his destiny in grand style.

Since we believe in the potency of names, my husband and I gave David the Ibo name Chikadibia for a reason. The name means: "God is greater than doctors." Indeed, who is it that says and it comes to pass when the Lord commanded it not **(Lamentations 3:37).** God is the author and the finisher of our faith and it is only His counsel that will stand in our lives. We give Him all the glory.

## Restore

After the birth of David, my husband and I decided that we didn't want any more children, given the trauma associated with my preg-nancies and the ten miscarriages I had in trying to have children. We decided to begin strict birth control. To ensure that we got it right, we approached the Johns Hopkins family planning clinic.

After consultations, the doctor told us that the most effective mode of birth control at that time was Ortho Evra, which is a proges-tin medication used as a method of birth control for women. It is used as a patch applied to the skin weekly. I was told that it was about 92 percent to 99.7 percent effective in preventing pregnancy and highly recommended. So, I settled for Ortho Evra. I was diligent in the usage of the patch under the unrelenting supervision of my husband. I never omitted using a patch on the appointed day.

Shortly after David turned one year in January 2005, I discovered that I was pregnant again. My husband was very upset about this fact in view of the sufferings associated with my pregnancies. We checked and rechecked the usage of the Ortho Evra and I had used the patches as prescribed. It was a very tense period in our household. In the midst of the tension, God spoke.

Two weeks after I discovered I was pregnant, my husband went to the basement of our home to pray in the early hours of one morning and God spoke to him concerning the baby. He told me that God reprimanded him, reminding him that we had specifically requested for three children, two boys and one girl, and the baby on the way was the girl we asked for. Therefore, the baby had to come even in spite of diligent birth control. He said God told him the baby should be called **Restore**.

When he got this instruction he thought God was referring to restoration in terms of the book of **Joel 2:25.** He was wrong, because God took him directly to the book of Isaiah and showed him the origin of the name **Restore** from **Isaiah 42:22.** That was the first time we ever saw that scripture, which states: **"But this is a people robbed and spoiled; they are all of them snared in holes, and they are hid in prison houses: they are for a prey, and none delivereth; for a spoil, and none saith, <u>Restore</u>"** (emphasis mine).

If you notice the spelling of the word Restore in this scripture starts with a capital letter R, signifying a name, as opposed to the book of Joel. God was telling us through this scripture that our days of suffering to have children were over. He had come to deliver us from the holes, snares, and prison where the devil had held us captive, robbing, spoiling, and preying on us.

Forever the scriptures cannot be broken. Restore's pregnancy was the easiest I ever had. Even though the doctors had tried to suggest to us that the fetus had abnormalities, we completely ignored them. We did not waste our thought on any negative medical verdict. We had a living testimony in David of just how God can change any negative situation. So, we believed completely that He who brought the baby would complete the work He started. The pregnancy was completely stress free—no bleeding, no sickness, no strict bed rests. I was driving my car all over Maryland conducting my business, which required a lot of socializing.

In the early hours of the morning of 7 October 2005, I felt a little discomfort in my lower back. We proceeded to the hospital where the doctors said I was in the early stages of labour. I was told the baby was still a long way coming, likely in the evening. I was admitted into the hospital around 7:30 a.m. My husband left for home to make arrangements for the care of David and John. Around 8:50 a.m., I suddenly felt pressure in my pelvic area. I called for the nurses. While the nurses were still trying to examine me, Restore's head popped out. She was delivered, wailing at the top of her lungs at precisely 8:58 a.m. I had delivered like the Hebrew women.

When I called my husband to tell him that the baby had arrived, he was very surprised. We named her Restore-Esther Chidera Awo. Chidera is an Ibo name which means "what God has ordained must come to pass." Restore is currently fifteen years old and is in grade ten at the International School of Brussels, Belgium. I call her the topping on my ice cream. She is very beautiful, talented, highly intelligent, and sings like a pro. She has plans of doing many things which include becoming a lawyer like her mother. She is an independent-minded person who voices her opinion come what may and a real crusader for the underserved. I know she will actualize her destiny and be an amazement to her generation.

*David at six months*

*David at two years and three months*

*David at sixteen years*

*Restore at four months*

*Restore at six months*

*Restore at fifteen years*

CHAPTER **8**

# Testimonies

*The righteousness of thy testimonies are everlasting;*
*give me understanding, and I shall live.*
**—Psalms 119:144**

WHATEVER WE ARE going through, we must continue to acknowledge and thank God for His previous acts in our lives. When we do this, we move His hands to perfect His plan and purpose for us. As Bishop Oyedepo says: "Every testimony is a seed; when you share it, you sow it and when you sow it, you get more testimonies because it turns into a harvest." Additionally, our testimonies of God's goodness are pointers to our heritage in Christ and are also weapons of warfare to overcome the devil (**Revelation 12:11**).

With the profound statement above in mind and with the conviction that testimonies have the power to replicate, I share a few of the many testimonies of how our children have devastated the yokes of barrenness and miscarriage. They are indeed for signs and wonders, arrows in the hands of a mighty man, here to torment the kingdom of darkness. These testimonies shall be replicated in the life of anyone that keys into them with faith and understanding in Jesus' name, Amen.

When David was born, my family was worshipping in a church called Restoring Life International Church, in Maryland. This was due to the fact that there was no Winners' Chapel Church in Maryland in those days. The day David was dedicated in church, we shared the testimony of his birth. After the testimony, the pastor, by divine direction, asked all the women in the church who were waiting on the Lord for the fruit of the womb to come out and carry the baby. My husband and I stood in front of the church with David while the women lined up and took turns carrying him. Thereafter, the church experienced a wave of pregnancies and births by women who had been called barren. One of these women was a sister in the choir who had suffered some miscarriages before this encounter. She took in shortly after the encounter; the pregnancy was preserved and she gave birth to a baby girl called Hannah.

In 2006 my family relocated back to The Gambia at the end of my husband's stint at the Johns Hopkins establishment. My husband was consulted by a couple in The Gambia who had been married for years and were said to be barren. After examining the laboratory and radiological results, every parameter was surprisingly within normal limits. Being a Christian armed with our testimonies, my husband told them that though there seemed to be no obvious medical problems, there could be spiritual challenges with spiritual solutions. He went ahead and shared our testimonies with the couple, referred them to our house to make contact with David, and called me to expect them.

Thereafter, the couple rushed to the house with excitement, but David was sleeping. The couple waited patiently and after a while I had compassion on them. I went and carried David in his sleepy state to the couple. Each of them hugged and carried David enthusiastically and passionately and left after a while. That same month, the woman conceived and subsequently had a baby boy whom they promptly named David as well.

Also, when I was seconded by the Commonwealth Secretariat London, UK, as a judge to the High Court of Swaziland, from 2010 to 2014, I met a man who, after I shared my testimony of childbirth with, informed me that he had been married for some years without children. He said his wife was also having miscarriages. He introduced his wife to me. That was the beginning of a great friendship with his family, which subsists until date. I asked him to come to my home and carry David and Restore with faith in his heart. He did as I instructed. A few months later the wife became pregnant. The pregnancy was miraculously preserved and she was delivered of a beautiful baby girl also called Restore. The siege of miscarriage was broken and the couple have since then had another baby girl called Esther.

Then, there is the interpreter in Winners' Chapel, Congo Brazzaville. When this testimony occurred, my husband was working with the World Health Organization (WHO) and was based at the WHO Regional Office for Africa in Congo Brazzaville, from 2012 to 2018. Given that he is an associate pastor in Winners' Chapel, having been ordained as such in March 2009, his testimony on childbirth was well known to the other pastors in the church. When I visited Congo Brazzaville with David and Restore, one of the pastors, Pastor Joko, informed my husband that one of the female interpreters in the church was under the siege of barrenness. Pastor Joko asked if it was possible for the lady and her husband to have contact with our children. My husband agreed.

So, after service on the appointed day, we met with the couple in the church conference room. They carried both children while we shared some scriptures, testimonies, and words of encouragement with them for about twenty minutes. We concluded with a short prayer. Within the same year, the interpreter conceived, the pregnancy was preserved, and she brought forth a bouncing baby boy. The siege of barrenness was broken and she had another baby boy this year in the midst of the COVID-19 pandemic.

# Epilogue

## Hoeilaart, Belgium, July, 2020

IT BEGAN AS a rumour.

Some called it a hoax.

Others said "Oh some Wuhan virus, a Chinese virus."

It was a China problem. This was the greatest error in judgment the world has ever made. By proceeding in the way and manner we proceeded, we forgot that the world is a global village, very connected. The tides turned very fast and COVID-19 (COVID), came knocking on the doors of Europe. Many began to die in the thousands and fear gripped all the nations. The palpable anxiety and the lockdowns commenced.

In Belgium, my children's school, the International School of Brussels, shut down on 9 March 2020 because of a suspected case of COVID in the school. Subsequently, Belgium went on lockdown on 18 March 2020. On Friday 20 March 2020, two days after Belgium was locked down, I woke up around 2:00 a.m. to relieve myself and I heard my daughter, Restore, coughing in her room upstairs. This made no impact on me until daybreak, when the cough persisted.

Restore began to complain of muscle pains, a lump in her throat, tightness in the chest, headaches, and fatigue. Indeed, she spent the whole day in bed. Considering that her school had shut down in the first place because of a suspected case of COVID in her grade, red lights immediately went off in my head.

I had gathered enough information from my husband, the internet, and the television on the symptoms of COVID to be concerned about Restore's symptoms. The following day my husband developed extreme fatigue, a persistent cough, and shortness of breath. I followed suit with muscle pains, enlarged lymph nodes, ear pain, vertigo, and conjunctivitis. I saw COVID staring us in the face and fear enveloped me.

On Monday 23 March 2020, during the prayer session (Covenant Hour of Prayer) for which we usually hook up on the internet to join our Prophet Bishop David Oyedepo, in Canaanland Ota, Nigeria, I heard clearly in my spirit: "Everyone is a victim of what he fears. Remember, they overcame him by the blood of the lamb and by the word of their testimony. Rather than wallow in fear why not testify, so that you and your household can overcome."

I thought the spirit instructed me to testify about my career path, the challenges faced and overcome. Therefore, immediately after the Covenant Hour of Prayer, I began to write my memoirs according to this understanding. However, I was mistaken, because as I laboured over the script, the voice of the Lord came again with clearer instructions: "Your testimony is long overdue. Testify for the world to see and be impacted. The Book shall be called *Children: My Heritage; A Testimony*.

I immediately informed my husband of this instruction and accordingly discarded the script on my career path, to testify as directed. As I wrote this testimony, all the COVID symptoms in my household disappeared speedily and of their own accord without any form of medication or hospitalization. May His name be praised.

It is clear from my testimony that satanic forces and oppressions are real and any battle of life with these forces can only be won on the platform of faith rooted in the word of God. On the wings of prophecy, the siege of miscarriages was broken and my first child came forth. Indeed, God works in mysterious ways, His wonders to perform. Active faith moved God's hand, and the womb that the doctors said should be removed because it was so impacted by fibroids that it could not hold any more babies, held two babies in quick succession.

My womb is still intact several years later. The persistent bleeding disappeared and the fibroids have vanished without a trace. The diabetes is gone forever. The babies we were told had abnormalities in the womb are perfectly normal and God is using them mightily in the area of childbirth. He is a covenant-keeping God. All we need is to fulfil our part of the covenant and He will do His own. As He says: *"My covenant will I not break, nor alter the thing that is gone out of my lips," Psalms 89:34.* We give Him all the glory.

The challenges I faced also taught me a lot of lessons, making me a stronger person and shaping me into the woman I am today. They prepared and positioned me to best weather other storms that life brought my way. Through my trials, I became more resilient and nimble to thread the needles of life. So, in all circumstances, I do not back down, holding unto Jesus the author and finisher of my faith. It is in Him I live, in Him I move, and in Him I have my being. Indeed, weeping may endure for a night but joy comes in the morning.

This testimony has been delayed because it is a very emotional journey for me. Severally, all through the years, I attempted to capture this testimony on paper. All my efforts proved abortive, overcome by emotions and tears. In this instance, the Holy Spirit enabled me to testify as instructed. He led me all the way till the end. My prayer is that anyone who has read this book with faith and understanding shall also experience a miracle. Thereby, turning their barrenness to fruitfulness, shame to fame, weeping to laughter, sorrows to joy, mourning to dancing, ashes to beauty, darkness to light, and trials to testimony in accordance with the scripture which states: *"Behold, at that time I will undo all that afflict thee: and I will save her that halted and gather her that was driven out; and I will get them praise and fame in every land where they have been put to shame," Zephaniah 3:19.*

AMEN

*My family Maryland USA 2006*

CPSIA information can be obtained
at www.ICGtesting.com
Printed in the USA
JSHW020155070421
13306JS00004B/8

9 781977 235060